MW01377795

WASHINGTON

WASHINGTON
Houses of the Capital

Photographs by Derry Moore
Text by Henry Mitchell
Foreword by Gore Vidal

A Studio Book   The Viking Press   New York

Copyright © 1982 by John Calmann & Cooper Ltd.
Photographs © 1982 by Derry Moore
Gore Vidal's foreword © 1982 by Literary Creation Enterprises, Inc.
This book was designed and produced by
John Calmann and Cooper Ltd., London

First published in 1982 by The Viking Press (A Studio Book)
625 Madison Avenue, New York, N.Y. 10022
Published simultaneously in Canada by
Penguin Books Canada Limited

Library of Congress Cataloging in Publication Data
Moore, Derry.
   Washington, houses of the Capital.
   (A Studio book)
   1. Architecture—Washington (D.C.)   2. Historic
buildings—Washington (D.C.)   3. Dwellings—Washington
(D.C.)   4. Embassy buildings—Washington (D.C.)
5. Washington (D.C.)—Buildings.   I. Mitchell,
Henry, 1923–   . II. Title.
NA735.W3M66   728'.09753   81-16292
ISBN 0-670-75006-9   AACR2

Printed in Hong Kong
Set in Great Britain

1. (*Frontispiece*) The stairway in the entrance lobby
of the Indonesian Embassy (the Walsh house).

Contents

Foreword by Gore Vidal

Like so many blind people my grandfather was a passionate sight-seer; not to mention a compulsive guide. One of my first memories is driving with him to a slum in southeast Washington. "All this," he said, pointing at the dilapidated red brick buildings, "was once our land." Since I saw only shabby buildings and could not imagine the land beneath, I was not impressed.

Years later I saw a map of how the District of Columbia had looked before the District's invention. Georgetown was a small community on the Potomac. The rest was farmland, owned by nineteen families. I seem to remember that the Gore land was next to that of the Notleys – a name that remains with me since my great-grandfather was called Thomas Notley Gore. Most of these families were what we continue to call – mistakenly – Scots-Irish. Actually, the Gores were Anglo-Irish from Donegal. They arrived in North America at the end of the seventeenth century and they tended to intermarry with other Anglo-Irish families – particularly in Virginia.

George Washington not only presided over the war of separation from Great Britain (revolution is much too strong a word for that confused and confusing operation) but he also invented the Federal republic whose original constitution reflected his powerful will to create the sort of government which would see to it that the rights of property will be forever revered. He was then congenial if not party to the deal that moved the capital of the new republic from the city of Philadelphia to the wilderness not far from his own Virginia estate.

When a grateful nation saw fit to call the capital-to-be Washington City, the great man made no strenuous demur. Had he not already established his modesty and republican virtue by refusing the crown of the new Atlantic nation on the ground that to replace George III with George I did not sound entirely right? Also, and perhaps more to the point, Washington had no children. There would be no Prince of Virginia, ready to ascend the rustic throne at Washington City when the founder of the dynasty was translated to a higher sphere.

Although Washington himself did not have to sell or give up any of his own land, he did buy a couple of lots as speculation. Then he died a year before the city was occupied by its first president-in-residence, John Adams. The families that had been dispossessed to make way for the capital city did not do too badly. The Gores who remained sold lots, built houses and hotels; and became rich. The Gores who went away – my grandfather's branch – moved to the far west, in those days, Mississippi. It was not until my grandfather was elected to the Senate in 1907 that he was able to come home again – never to leave until his death in 1949.

Although foreign diplomats enjoy maintaining that Washington is – or was – a hardship post, the British minister in 1809, one Francis James Jackson, had the good sense to observe, "I have procured two very good saddle horses, and Elizabeth and I have been riding in all directions round the place whenever the weather has been cool enough. The country has a beautifully picturesque appearance, and I have nowhere seen finer scenery than is composed by the Potomac and the woods and hills about it; yet it has a wild and desolated air from being so scantily and rudely cultivated, and from the want of population . . . So you see we are not fallen into a wilderness, – so far from it that I am surprised no one should before have mentioned the great beauty of the neighborhood. The natives trouble themselves but little about it; their thoughts are chiefly of tobacco, flour, shingles, and the news of the day." *Plus ça change.*

Twenty years ago, that well-known wit and man-about-town, John F. Kennedy, said, "Washington perfectly combines southern efficiency with northern charm." I think that this was certainly true of the era when he and his knights of the Round Table were establishing Camelot amongst the local chiggers. By then too many glass buildings were going up. Too many old houses were being torn down or allowed to crumble. Too many slums were metastasizing around Capitol Hill. Also, the pre-war decision to make an imperial Roman – literally, Roman – capital out of what had been originally a pleasant Frenchified Southern city was, in retrospect, a mistake.

I can remember that when such Roman palaces as the Commerce Department were being built, we used to wonder, rather innocently, how these huge buildings could ever be filled up with people. But a city is an organism like any other and an organism seems to know just what it has been encoded to be. Long before the American empire was a reality, the city was turning itself into New Rome. While the basilicas and porticoes were going up, one often had the sense that one was living not in a city that was being built but in a set of ruins. It is curious that even in those pre-nuclear days many of us could imagine the city devastated. Was this, perhaps, some memory of the War of 1812 when the British burned Capitol and White House? Or of the Civil War when Southern troops invaded the city, coming down Seventh Street Road?

"At least they will make wonderful ruins," said my grandfather, turning his blind eyes on the Archives Building; he was never a man to spend public money on anything if he could help it. But those Piranesi blocks of marble eventually became real buildings that soon filled up with real bureaucrats and by the end of the Second World War, Washington had a real world empire to go with all those (to my eyes, at least) bogus-Roman sets.

Empires are dangerous possessions, as Pericles was among the first to point out. Since I recall pre-imperial Washington, I am a bit of an old Republican in the Ciceronian mode, given to decrying the corruption of the simpler, saner city of my youth. In the twenties and thirties, Washington was a small town where everyone knew everyone else. When school was out in June, boys took off their shoes and did not put them on again – at least outside the house – until September. The summer heat was – and is –

Egyptian. In June, before Congress adjourned, I used to be sent with car and driver to pick up my grandfather at the Capitol and bring him home. In those casual days, there were few guards at the Capitol – and, again, everyone knew everyone else. I would wander onto the floor of the Senate, sit on my grandfather's desk if he wasn't ready to go, experiment with the snuff that was ritually allotted each senator; then I would lead him off the floor. On one occasion, I came down the aisle of the Senate wearing nothing but a bathing suit. This caused a good deal of amusement, to the blind man's bewilderment. Finally, the Vice President, Mr Garner – teeth like tiny black pearls and a breath that was all whiskey – came down from the chair and said, "Senator, this boy is nekkid." Afterwards I always wore a shirt on the Senate floor – but never shoes.

I date the end of the old republic and the birth of the empire to the invention, in the late thirties, of air-conditioning. Before air-conditioning, Washington was deserted from mid-June to September. The president – always Franklin Roosevelt – headed up the Hudson and all of Congress went home. The gentry withdrew to the northern resorts. Middle-income people flocked to Rehobeth Beach, Delaware – or Virginia Beach, which was slightly more racy. But after air-conditioning and the Second World War arrived, more or less at the same time, Congress sits and sits while the presidents – or at least their staffs – never stop making mischief at the White House or in the splendid old State and War Departments building, now totally absorbed by the minions of President Augustus. The Pentagon – a building everyone hated when it was being built – still gives us no great cause to love either its crude appearance or its function, so like that of a wasp's nest aswarm.

Now our Roman buildings are beginning to darken with time and pigeon droppings while the brutal glass towers of the late twentieth century tend to mask and dwarf them. But here and there in the city one still comes across shaded streets and houses; little changed from the last century and we are all in Derry Moore's debt for memorializing so many relics of lost time – when men wore white straw hats and suits in summer while huge hats decorated the ladies (hats always got larger just before a war) and one dined at Harvey's Restaurant where the slow-turning ceiling-fans and tessellated floors made the hottest summer day seem cool even though the air of the street outside was oven-like and smelled of jasmine and hot tar, while nearby Lafayette Park was a lush tropical jungle where one could see that Civil War hero, Mr Justice Oliver Wendell Holmes, stroll, his white moustaches unfurled like fierce battle pennants. At the park's edge our entirely own and perfectly unique Henry Adams held court for decades in a house opposite to that Executive Mansion where grandfather and great-grandfather had reigned over a capital that was little more than a village down whose muddy main street ran a creek that was known to some even then as – what else? – the Tiber.

Introduction

2 Brickwork detailing reminiscent of the French Renaissance attracts the eye, as do the striped awnings.

Washington is the capital of the United States. When the nation became an independent state in 1776 no town existed where the Capitol now is and numerous Americans doubted the prudence, or indeed the sanity, of establishing a capital on the Potomac River at the point where it falls from the Piedmont to the Tidewater flatlands. But far too many whines have been registered that Washington is a "goddam swamp," as a Speaker of the House of Representatives once asserted, merely because there was a bit of standing water at the site of the Lincoln Memorial. The dwellings of the city, as you will see in these pages, are not actually built on stilts, and the trifling circumstance that half the houses of the city have flooded basements when it rains is a reproach not to the excellent physical environment of the town, but to inept architects and builders.

People from London or Moscow regard the capital as a tropical encampment. They assume they will die of malaria or worse, and they believe they deserve hardship pay and the license to go naked except for a half-inch layer of insect repellent. How wrong these preconceptions are may be gauged by the fact that Southerners in the United States think of Washington as the extreme northern limit of the habitable world, and regard the Washington summers as too cool, too brief, too hostile for snowy egrets to flourish, and too near the Arctic for the blood to be properly thinned and purified by an honest sweat.

Washington is a few minutes from an arm of the Atlantic Ocean, the Chesapeake Bay, which does far more for crabs and oysters than for the tempering of the climate, which is essentially continental rather than maritime, simply because the weather moves in from the west across several thousand miles of buffalo and wilderness. In winter it is far colder than London and in summer it is very like Calcutta. These are the marks of a continental climate and they are relevant to the design of a house. Or should be.

In the southeastern coastal plain, for instance, which runs down from Norfolk in Virginia around the Gulf of Mexico into Texas and up the Mississippi River north of Memphis, the houses vary according to tradition and local building materials, but their great feature is a central hall running north and south the entire depth of the house. The rooms open

3 A Sixteenth Street mansion where music is honored and all but worshiped is full of pianos, but also astonishing harmonies of antique rugs, polished wood, brocade, gilded bronze; a natural habitat of the stuffed tiger. It is the Toutorsky house.

4 A surprise Christmas gift from his wife, this Sixteenth Street mini-palace once owned by President Taft's treasury secretary is now the Mexican Embassy. A fireplace hinting of Loire châteaux emphasizes the rather grand effect.

from this shady hall, which catches the breeze from the south. Such houses are cold in the winter, or were before central heating became standard, but it made no great difference since winter was a matter of a few days and the important thing was to remain cool throughout the long hot summer.

In Washington, however, the winter is not to be taken so lightly. It can freeze in October, though there may be some shirt-sleeve weather even in December, and even the end of May can be wet, chilly and miserable, causing the town's ubiquitous amateur gardeners to complain each year, as if newly outraged, that their roses and peonies are ruined. Indeed, torrential rains with or without lightning, thunder, wind and hail, are certain as the irises and the roses approach their greatest splendor.

Thunderstorms, by the way, alarm many visitors from abroad who are not used to them, except the British, who are also not used to them but who regularly display what Americans consider an unnatural and perhaps lunatic joy in crashing thunder and splintered trees.

Chilly weather holds on far into spring – though it is a rare April that does not have a day or two of heat into the nineties before returning to chilly or even frosty nights – and it is not desirable to have the house fully shaded by verandahs or galleries. These would be welcome during the capital's warm summers, but unacceptable and gloomy otherwise.

As late as the 1930s small houses were being built in Washington with walls of solid masonry (brick, as a rule) with no insulating air space. Such houses are surprisingly comfortable in summer, rarely requiring the air-conditioning system to be turned on, but almost impossible to warm up in winter. If it were not for central cooling and heating systems, more attention would certainly be paid to the importance of north-south air flow in houses, since Washington is sufficiently southern to benefit from it.

Some of the houses of this book were built, however, not as an architectural solution to the challenge of climate, but as statements of influence and assertions of power. One notable family built a notable house in Washington because they were assured Washington was warm. They visited in December, a remarkable December with balmy days, and they assumed they had discovered the Indies. What they thought during a sixteen-inch snow fall in February is not recorded.

The nature of the human beast is to complain of climate, a circumstance that should not blur the fact that sunny days are the rule, not the exception, in Washington. Winter skies are usually of an intense blue, and late summer and autumn can bring day after day of crystal light, temperatures in the eighties, and the air electric with the song of cicadas, as in the south of France. All of this leads to a cheerful spirit and is possibly the origin of American optimism and bounce.

Some of the most wonderful houses reflect this. There is an innocence about many of them that is disarming: a cereal heiress might see nothing odd in hanging enormous portraits of Catherine the Great in her entrance

5 This example of decorative brickwork indicates something of the complexity of detail than can be achieved with a few basic elements.

7 Victorian houses once ignored are now properly honored. Most were soundly built and worked with care and skill as this redbrick detail testifies.

6 Ground-beetles live in a fairyland of whirling spectrums much of the summer when the White House lawn sprinklers operate. The north portico looks out, towards the left, to a fountain and beds of flowers, and beyond to a tall iron fence separating it from the tourists, protesters and general traffic of Pennsylvania Avenue.

8 Without warning, the foot traveller comes on houses virtually untouched by changing fashions, like this gingerbread gem with its wonderful fretwork arch beneath the eaves of the patterned roof. The color scheme is a bit novel but the old iron gate is standard.

9 A pair of houses designed to present the appearance of a somewhat larger establishment have the steep roofs and windows above cornice level that give the flavour of a French château.

hall, and another more modest grande dame may ask you in 1981 if you think the woodwork should be repainted since its last coat in 1928 – it still looks brand new, incredibly enough, but it seems rather a long while between paint jobs. Then there is the house-proud lawyer whose house, he insists, is a full eleven feet wide, and you hesitate to get out the yardstick and prove to him it's only ten. Pianos shipped from France have had roomier quarters in their packing crates, but the man, whose entire house is smaller than many a bedroom elsewhere, supposes his place is very like Louis XIV's château at Marly. A little bit smaller, yes, but by no means too small.

The house of a former Secretary of the Navy has nice fanlights in the doors and all seems normal. You begin to notice a lavish assortment of toy trains all over the place. For man cannot live by fanlights alone. A man exerts himself immeasurably on his house in Washington and his wife arrives from France, takes one look and is out the door. It is commonly said that it was her own cool reception in Washington which prompted her abrupt departure, but her husband was left with the house. What had been intended to provide his greatest happiness was now a reminder of

10 A terrace of houses is enlivened by the use of alternating gabled dormers and porticoes.

11, 12 Although in obvious decay there is just enough decorative detail in the brackets and around the windows to indicate that these were once prosperous middle-class houses (*left*). Wrought-iron work (*right*) looks particularly effective here in dappled sunlight.

misery. Well, these things happen. People can be very strange. A senator lives in a house once occupied by a physician who treated some of the British soldiers wounded at the Battle of Bladensburg, in the suburbs, on August 24, 1814. He was so good to them they gave him a gold snuffbox. Then they proceeded right along and burnt the Capitol and White House.

These ironies and these tangents are not, of course, peculiar to Washington and its houses, but are rather the essential stuff of human history everywhere, which is why, no doubt, one warms so quickly to the houses of this capital. Somehow it is plainer to see in this town.

The first capital was New York, where George Washington was sworn in as first president in 1789, but there had been heated arguments over where to site it ever since 1783 when the Congress first determined to establish a Federal City. Philadelphia had seemed the likely location since it had been the seat of the Continental Congresses during the Revolution, and was conveniently placed between New England and Virginia, the dominant American powers of the day. But Philadelphia was a Quaker

19

13, 14 Every effort has been made to give these houses (*below*) their own identity by varying the roof shapes, materials and fenestration. Octagonal wings (*right*) create a rather heavy effect.

city and Virginia was Anglican. and even more to the point, the South darkly suspected that if the capital were permanently fixed in Pennsylvania the Quaker sentiment against slavery would soon be reflected in national policy to the detriment of slave holders in the South. The matter came to a head when, after all had been said, the capital had to be put somewhere, and a ten-mile square located partly in Maryland and partly in Virginia was chosen.

Readers familiar with American political processes will not imagine it was chosen because it was the best site, or because the citizens of the new republic felt an overwhelming fondness for it. On the contrary, hardly anybody had ever dreamed of it, let alone heard of it, and the selection came about as a compromise over something else. The something else was a proposal – or a diabolical scheme as the South regarded it – of Alexander Hamilton's, by which the new republic would take over the debts the states had accumulated in pursuing the Revolution. Commercial interests of the northeastern seaboard were keen for the national government to assume these debts, but the southern seaboard, largely agricultural, was decidedly unenthusiastic.

Thomas Jefferson observed at the time that this question was the severest test of national unity yet to face the new country. Hamilton's proposal

failed in the Congress, thanks to Southern votes against it, and there was talk of secession by the commercial states even before the new country was well launched in the world. Hamilton was dismayed at the failure of his plan, which he regarded as the only feasible one, but Jefferson and the South generally saw it as a ploy of the Northern commercial interests to protect their investments in state bonds which they had bought at discount from the original owners.

Jefferson finally arranged a meeting with Hamilton at which an historic compromise was reached: the South would reconsider its opposition and accept in general the terms of the Hamilton plan. Hamilton, in exchange, would agree to establishing the capital in the South.

Congress, after some more wrangling, authorized President Washington himself to select a site on the Potomac River. Scarcely a dwelling existed there at the time; apart from the tobacco ports of Alexandria and George-town, all the acres on which government buildings now stand were merely farmland or woods.

President Washington's farm, Mount Vernon, lies in the suburbs of present-day Washington, but the evil-minded should know that the president owned no land in what is now the capital. Quite apart from being the father of the new nation, and probably the only man of his time in America who could have held the loose family of sovereign states together in any sort of unity in the eighteenth century, George Washington was also eminently practical in small matters. He himself haggled, if that is not a disrespectful word, with those who owned the land in 1790, pointing out to them how lucky they were that their mere farms had been chosen to become a great capital.

Although the site of Washington was somewhat a wilderness, it was a privately owned wilderness. At the time of the first permanent settlement

15, 16, 17, 18 More examples of attractive brickwork detailing. On the left the change of detail below cornice level at the junction of the flat wall and rounded tower is not entirely satisfactory. A happier resolution can be seen in the house on the right, where the cornice runs around the tower and attaches it firmly to the main part of the building.

of Virginia, at Jamestown in 1607, Algonquin Indians lived in what is now Washington. Seventeenth-century maps show the entire area so full of place names that they resemble detailed maps of modern Surrey and Kent. These names pinpointed Indian settlements. The site of the present city was visited in 1608 by John Smith from the Jamestown settlement. His map of 1612, published in London, must have encouraged later settlers, sprinkled as it was with dozens of place names which, though unpronounceable, such as Nameroughquend (where the Pentagon now stands), at least indicated that humans could live in the place, and indeed that they had found it sufficiently desirable to want to construct villages everywhere.

As early as 1590 a brochure had appeared in London explaining how delightful it would be to settle in America with other Englishmen. John White's drawings, at the (ultimately unsuccessful) Roanoke Island settlement being drummed up by Sir Walter Raleigh, show Indians dancing in a circle in apparent delight, holding hands and largely naked, while others wander over to a feast of fish and three large salvers of obviously delectable (unnamed) viands, or cavort through a sort of park shooting deer with arrows. In the background an Indian gentleman sits on a raised platform guarding a plantation of corn (Zea mays) against birds and exotic beasts by emitting "continual cryes and noyse." But lest any intending settler should get the idea that constant guarding of everything was necessary, Mr White assured his readers that the Indians are "voyde of all covetousness" and "lyve cherfullye and at their harts ease."

This paradise was carved into royal patents (Lord Baltimore petitioned King Charles I for his lands in what is now Maryland in 1629) and the lands were subdivided. Lord Culpepper and the Earl of Arlington received vast grants of Virginian lands in 1673. There was of course some confusion when it turned out that Englishmen were already settled on some of these lands thus cavalierly given by the Crown, but by the end of the seventeenth century all of what is now Washington was in private hands.

One obstinate (the adjective is George Washington's) Scotsman, Davy Burns, had a farm he did not want to part with, capital or no capital, and General Washington had trouble persuading him, finally pointing out that if Burns did not willingly agree to give up the land, the nation could simply condemn it. Besides, the general reasoned with the farmer, he would become a rich man since he would give half the land, laid off in building lots, to the government but would retain the other half and make a fortune from their sale. The general, who occasionally may have failed in tact, told Burns that if it were not for the selection of these lands as part of the capital, Burns would live and die a poor tobacco farmer. To which Burns retorted that if Washington had not married the rich Widow Custis with all her black slaves Washington would have lived and died a poor land surveyor. Burns yielded to necessity, and by 1792 was advertising his building lots in the new city with enthusiasm: "A purchaser may combine prospect, commercial advantage and vicinity to the President's Palace."

The lands of the District of Columbia had been owned by nineteen farming families, many of them related by marriage. Throughout the eighteenth century these lands kept being transferred through death, marriage and various settlements, and while some families did make money selling building lots, most did not, for the obvious reason that a new capital in a wilderness has to become a real city before the land is worth much. President Washington foresaw that the capital of the United States was bound to become a major city – as indeed it did after a couple of centuries – and he had the vision to demand a great plan for it, lest it grow like Topsy.

A French major, Pierre L'Enfant, drew the plans which, surprisingly enough (surprising to Americans), have been largely followed, consisting of a grid of north-south and east-west streets, enlivened (especially at the traffic circles from which they radiate) by great diagonal avenues. L'Enfant was sometimes reproached for having delusions of grandeur, but Jefferson was among those who kept prodding him to make the avenues even wider.

It must not be supposed that once the great plan for the city was finished all went swimmingly. The plan was all very splendid, but of course it was unclear where the money to implement it would come from. One of the commissioners appointed by Washington to arrange for the land had a grand house that inconveniently was smack in the middle of one of L'Enfant's grand avenues. L'Enfant had the mansion torn down before the commissioner was aware of what was going on. History universally suggests that employees who tear down their employer's mansions without so much as a by-your-leave will often encounter opposition. The commissioner appealed to President Washington who fired L'Enfant. Great radiating avenues are all very well and Washington himself loved them, but that does not give a city planner license to operate like a madman.

19 Plasterwork such as this evokes a feeling of past splendors.

In the end the avenue went where L'Enfant wanted it, but he did not fare well in a worldly way, and in his old age used to wander about the capital like a lost soul. A somewhat graceless complex of buildings, called L'Enfant Plaza, has recently been named in his honor, but his chief memorial is the great axis from the Capitol to the Lincoln Memorial, malls lined with double avenues of trees and excellent museums and reflecting pools, as well as with tourists and joggers in their running shorts.

John Adams was the first president to settle into the new capital after all the government papers and paraphernalia were shipped down from Philadelphia. His wife Abigail has left an account of her travels to the city in November 1800: "Having lost my way in the woods on Saturday in going from Baltimore, we took the road to Frederick and got nine miles out of our road. You find nothing but a Forest and woods on the way, for 16 and 18 miles not a village. Here and there a thatched cottage, without a single pane of glass . . ." She expected to find "trees and stumps in plenty" and indeed found them, along with God's own amplitude of virgin mud.

20 Decorative ironwork was often mass-produced but still looks attractive even when neglected.

21 All is in better order here and handsome brickwork is again in evidence.

As she was a woman of refinement she did not dwell in any unwholesome way on these things, contenting herself with the observation that "the country around is romantic, but a wild, a wilderness at present."

The port towns of Georgetown and Alexandria were both part of the District of Columbia's hundred-square-mile area, but for decades they regarded themselves as quite separate from Washington itself. Alexandria, on the Virginia side of the Potomac, boasted some pretty eighteenth-century houses, as did Georgetown, which by 1820 had some three hundred brick dwellings, and in comparison with the cuckoo's egg of Washington in the same nest the two towns felt themselves somewhat better feathered, but the burgeoning newcomer soon reduced them to unimportance.

Alexandria, which might itself have been selected as the capital had it not been for George Washington's disinclination to choose his own home town, or an area in which he had substantial real estate holdings and personal interests, was given back to Virginia in 1846. Georgetown only became part of Washington in 1871, when the agreeable names of its 27

22 Another example of a row of houses given individuality by variation in detail.

streets (such as Wapping and Duck) were reduced to unimaginative and convenient designations like Thirtieth and P Streets, but it remains, in the view of Georgetowners, the most desirable place to live.

"There appeared to be but two really comfortable habitations, in all respects, within the bounds of the city," an observer wrote in 1800. One of these was owned by a gentleman named Notley Young, and as it happened it was in the way of one of L'Enfant's grand boulevards. L'Enfant asked the commissioners, his employers, to remove the Young house since it was "a nuisance to the city," but at least he didn't summarily tear it down. General Washington, who had lived through the storm occasioned by L'Enfant's earlier removal of a nuisance, felt no need to endure another one. He intervened and the Young house remained standing, only to be demolished in 1856. It may seem remarkable that with so few houses in the city, L'Enfant kept trying to run avenues through them. It must have taken some skill to design streets that would hit a house.

An observer of 1804 took the usual happy American view of the new metropolis: "We only need here houses, cellars, kitchens, scholarly men, amiable women, and a few other such trifles, to possess a perfect city." The Secretary of the Treasury, Albert Gallatin, said the same thing less sweetly, as befitted a financier: "Our local situation is far from being pleasant or even convenient. Around the Capitol are seven or eight board-

23 An attractive bow window is only slightly marred by the flat glazing.

ing houses, one tailor, one shoemaker, one printer, a washing woman, a grocery shop, a pamphlets and stationery shop, a small dry goods shop and an oyster house. This makes the whole of the Federal City ...'' One can but wonder what else he could desire. All the same, he was not alone in finding the new capital lacking in glory, even with its 3,000 inhabitants. Many government officials lived in boarding houses, not bringing their families with them. There were only 127 government clerks at the time; however, they seem to have had numerous descendants, judging by the present number.

The British burned the capital's public buildings in the War of 1812 and while the architect Latrobe said this was the most splendid benefit (since people saw the capital being rebuilt and thus had confidence in its permanence, and everybody began building a new house) some citizens did not think it so great a blessing. Renewed cries went up that the capital should be moved, not only to a militarily safer site, but also to one more free of swamp fever. The United States Congress, not always consistent in its decisions, has yet held firm on the matter of the capital. Either loyalty or inertia kept the capital where George Washington put it and now even cautious seers generally believe it will remain on the Potomac for the foreseeable future.

As time passed, the city grew to supply the needs of the government,

with spurts in population following wars. Today about three million people live in Washington and its suburbs, and bureaucracy has expanded accordingly. If you want to run a train under the metropolis you will meet with various jurisdictions: the Federal Government, the District of Columbia Government, the state governments of Maryland and Virginia, and the various county governments of Montgomery, Fairfax, and Prince George's. Taxes, zoning laws, traffic regulations and building codes, among other things, all vary somewhat, though it is a universal sentiment that things are cheaper and more efficient in all jurisdictions other than where one happens to live.

Within the bounds of the city itself, 70 per cent of the citizens are black, but the relative proportion of whites and blacks in the metropolitan area has remained stable throughout the capital's history – 65 per cent white and 35 per cent black. Washington was a major center of the slave trade, which was only abolished in the capital in 1850, but even before the Civil War of 1861 black freedmen composed 78 per cent of the black population.

As late as the end of the 1930s the capital was regarded as a Southern town, in which wrinkled cotton seersucker suits were the uniform for summer, and a certain leisureliness was expected at all times (especially by those doing business with the Federal Government). Now it may have changed somewhat, though New Yorkers still make it a point to annoy citizens of Washington by remarking on the "slow pace" of the capital.

Up until the present century ordinary citizens used to drop in at the White House to call on the president, and when a president held open house it was indeed open to everybody. Mrs Taft's well-known spotted cow, Pauline, happily chomped on the White House lawn until it was moved in 1912 (to the considerable displeasure of Mrs Taft) to Foggy Bottom where the State Department is now. Mrs Taft made arrangements for the cow to be brought up every day and returned to its stable in the afternoon by a schoolchild.

One trembles a little at sailing through the sea of Washington history in so slender a chapter, it is as if one were to wrap up England from Caesar to Churchill in a thousand words or so, and one might well remark on the presence of Pauline, the Taft cow, and the absence here of Abraham Lincoln's assassination. But Lincoln, the prince of all American heroes, tells us little of the course of Washington houses and Pauline, gnawing contentedly on the magnolias, tells something.

However, nothing is more irksome than for a book to start apologizing for defects and omissions (as if the readers could not perfectly well find them out for themselves) so let there be no further cringing here. You have before you a loving survey of Washington houses that for one reason or another seemed wonderful or lovely or unbelievable or crazy (or all four) to a photographer and a writer, who shed no blood to speak of in their choices of what to show and tell.

24 A fine stone-carved ram's head capital with oak leaf decoration looks down a little mournfully, but makes a splendid detail.

31

The Eighteenth Century

The cornerstone of the White House was laid in 1792 after the usual fits and starts common to the American capital. General Washington had assumed that the designer of the city's plan, Major Pierre L'Enfant, would not merely lay out the streets and plazas but also design such important buildings as the Capitol and the President's house.

Somewhat less than a year after he had been hired, L'Enfant had picked the site for the Capitol and the White House (as the President's house is now called) and had laid out the right-angled street grid, cut by diagonal avenues. But he had not, for some reason, designed any major buildings. General Washington, who himself spent decades converting the "little oblong box left him by his brother into the noble mansion" admired by many – that is, his own dwelling, Mount Vernon, a few miles in the country beyond the capital – should perhaps have had some sympathy for him. L'Enfant, however, within a year was expected to design a new city, and its principal buildings, more important and more graceful than General Washington's farm mansion.

L'Enfant set to work on his plan in March 1791, and promptly tangled with two of the three commissioners appointed by General Washington to oversee the new capital. Within a year, Washington felt obliged to suspend L'Enfant from his post. The truth is that while L'Enfant's tardiness may have been cited as an objection, his inability to get along with important men was the true reason for his suspension.

Since L'Enfant had failed to produce designs for the White House, a competition was held, and was won by James Hoban. Some remarkable entries were received, although General Washington observed in a letter, as the July 1792 deadline neared, that if nothing better turned up than the designs he was aware of, the results were going to be very dull indeed.

Thomas Jefferson, smitten by the twin glories of Rome and of Palladio, had already given much valuable free advice to L'Enfant on the general layout of the city, and modestly submitted a design for the White House under a pseudonym. His design, not surprisingly, bore a strong resemblance both to Palladio's Villa Rotonda and to his own house, Monticello. Naturally it was crowned by a dome, since Jefferson believed a domeless

25 In the White House a portrait of George Washington, the first president, is reflected in a Federal-period mirror; an Indian chief, a Chinese porcelain lamp, an elegant caned settee reflect the taste of the early republic.

life was not worth living, and, moreover, his dome cascaded with skylights; the dome was really ribs interspersed with skylights. The design did not win. There is no doubt, however, that if it had prevailed, the White House, by the time it was actually translated into reality from Jefferson's initial design, would have been more ingenious and surprising than the structure we know from Hoban.

Hoban was an Irish architect who had already designed the capitol building of South Carolina. His winning design for the White House suggests Leinster House in Dublin, and has much of the charm and slender elegance associated with Irish Palladian efforts. Jefferson, possibly con-

26 Glimpsed through trees the White House has an air of quiet grandeur.

vinced his own design was better, said of Hoban's White House that it was "a great stone house, big enough for two emperors, one pope, and the grand lama." The entrance hall of the White House measures 28 by 44 feet. The entrance hall of Jefferson's own Monticello is 24 by 32 feet. The drawing room of the White House is 28 by 39 feet; Jefferson's country-house drawing room is just over 24 by 28 feet. The comparison speaks for itself: the White House is not disproportionately larger than Jefferson's own dwelling. And, of course, more gatherings were likely to be held in the house of the American president than in a gentleman's farmhouse.

The British burned the White House and Capitol in 1814, five years after Jefferson completed his terms as president; otherwise, he might have seized the chance to rebuild the White House himself. As it was, since the house was big enough for two emperors, a pope and a lama, Jefferson corrected this defect by enlarging it with twin terraces at either end, on which countless cubic feet have been added to the original building.

Jefferson also got his way (though only after his death) when the handsome north portico, which bears an uncanny resemblance to the original Jefferson proposal for the house, was added by Benjamin Latrobe whom he had made Surveyor of Public Works. The garden front also blossomed forth with a semi-circular portico (as Jefferson wished) instead of the modest flat row of columns designed by Hoban.

Abigail Adams, first of the presidents' wives to live in the house (in 1800), had laundry hung in the East Room. It is not airy enough for this purpose today but perhaps it was then. She also noted that the grand stairway was unfinished.

The East Room, which measures 39 by 80 feet, with a 22-foot-high ceiling, is painted cream with gilt touches, and has some vast chandeliers and handsome portraits of General and Mrs Washington. It is the usual site of the "Entertainments" which follow dinners given by the president and his wife. Some 350 people may be invited for the entertainment, in addition to those invited for dinner, and these invitations are prized and rarely declined.

Guests arrive through some pretty rooms on the lower level, admiring china and plate in lighted glass cabinets, and proceed along a spacious basement corridor lined with portraits of presidents' wives, and up stairs which debouch into a small hall off the main entrance lobby. This leads to the East Room, where they are invited to sit on rather small gilt chairs. The president and his party enter and the whole room is then treated to whatever entertainment the president has authorized. It might be a strident soprano. It might be worse. It might even be better. In any case it makes no great difference, since guests lap up the glory of merely being there, never mind what the entertainment is or, for that matter, who the president is. Afterwards, everybody mills about in the lovely public rooms, sometimes plopping down heavily on antique chairs, sometimes even moving mantel ornaments given by President Madison. Curators are banned from these evening festivities in the interest of preventing their heart attacks.

If you light a cigarette in the Oval Drawing Room a waiter commonly appears from nowhere with an embarrassingly large receptacle for you to drop ashes in. They understand, those stewards, that barbarians are often in the house and are somewhat resigned to it. They do not propose, however, to see the house burnt down again.

Over the generations the house has been redecorated from time to time. Almost every First Lady, as the president's wife has come to be called, walks in the door, takes one look at the place, silently deplores the taste of her immediate predecessor and calls in a decorator. Nowadays it is chiefly the private apartments upstairs that get a royal going over with each new incumbent. Mrs Kennedy, however, also installed some wallpaper trim beneath the cornices of the main downstairs rooms.

Portraits are also moved about. Benjamin Franklin or Thomas Jefferson may be demoted from their lofty positions of prominence and Calvin Coolidge exalted. Another administration takes over, and things may reverse. Presidents Washington and Lincoln are both fairly secure, no matter who the incumbent may be.

There was a time, mercifully past and forgotten, in which the White House flowered with ghastly Victorian mantels and stuffed ottomans, and resembled a blend of Crystal Palace and Aunt Emily's little Turkish corner with plenty of palms and peacock feathers. During the Truman regime the building was gutted, structural members were rebuilt and the rooms replaced. This has been the only major renovation since 1814.

The rooms are now, and for some years have been, back to their original late eighteenth- and early nineteenth-century appearance, or at least what we think was their appearance then. We can get some idea of how blinkered we are in our views of past architectural styles by observing any restoration project a century later; we wonder how the restorers could have been so blind and so faithless to the original style. And yet in our own day, when we ourselves do it, we rather admire our skill at recreating a room or a building in the idiom of the past.

The White House, mercifully Palladian in style, differs from the usual Maryland and Virginia eighteenth-century house. However, like them, it takes its architectural decoration – its dentils, ovolos, pilasters and modillions – seriously. Its cornices and mouldings are dutifully, even exuberantly, presented, and the eighteenth-century American fondness for luxury of display is maintained. Nevertheless, a certain cleanness and simplicity is sensed in the interior as a whole. The earlier mansions of Virginia and Maryland fairly shout their craftsmanship at you as you enter, but the White House is far more subdued.

There are other earlier American houses in which the very baseboards are elaborated and carved (in Gunston Hall they project four inches into the room). In such a house as Marmion (about 1670) you could scarcely walk two paces in the drawing room (installed in 1735) without meeting a carved Ionic pilaster. The room is fully paneled with complete Ionic entablature. Furthermore, the panels are themselves painted with landscapes, urns, and garlands. Similarly, Stratford (1725) boasts superb paneling of full Corinthian order in its main hall. Its proportions may not be entirely academic, but in elaboration and splendor it far surpasses the later taste of the century seen in the White House.

Dozens of examples could be cited, not only from Virginia and Maryland (Virginia surpassed the other colonies in the general costliness and lavishness of its houses), but from Carolina, Pennsylvania (where a certain rightness and polish is the expected thing), New York, Massachusetts, Vermont, and even Maine.

The eighteenth-century American ideal was to build as grandly as could possibly be managed. Occasionally a house like Rosewell (1726) brought substantial financial difficulty to the family that built it, but no matter: the perfection of the brickwork, the cut-stone chimney cornices, the magnificent carving of the great staircase, should be sufficient recompense.

The typical Virginia country house consisted of a central block with two or more dependent blocks in a forecourt, either unconnected with the main house or else joined by colonnades. In harsher climates the outbuildings became connected wings, and in New England the house was usually one central block.

Dumbarton House – not to be confused with Dumbarton Oaks – is an eighteenth-century house that found itself in the middle of Q Street (George Beall, who is believed to have built the original house, protested in 1750 that his property might be "totally demolished" if the new town of Georgetown were allowed to expand on its established grid) and was therefore moved a short distance to its present location on O Street in 1915. It is now a museum, and headquarters of the National Society of Colonial Dames, and open to the public.

The present house has two dependent blocks connected with the main building by enclosed passageways. An exceptional feature of the central block is the pair of twin rooms that project to the back in semi-circular bays, a novel if not unique treatment for the period. The interior trim is far less elaborate than in earlier Virginia houses and the cornices have an Adamesque delicacy rather than the carved wooden full classical entablatures that might be expected. This is no doubt because the house was rebuilt in 1805. Already taste was changing, and the rich sober fully articulated paneling typical of eighteenth-century American mansions was giving way to a new lightness. City dwellings, notably in Georgetown (once a separate town, it will be recalled, though now almost in downtown Washington), became simpler and, as later examples will show, quite narrow mouldings began to be used; even when cost was not a primary

27 The entrance hall of Dumbarton House, now the headquarters of the National Society of Colonial Dames, creates a feeling of lightness and elegance.

37

consideration, ceiling cornices were often omitted entirely. But en route to this new simplicity, both the White House and Dumbarton House are stops along the way.

A most interesting eighteenth-century house is The Lindens, built in 1754 in Danvers, Massachusetts. It was scheduled for demolition but fortunately rescued by its present owner, who moved it to Washington in 1934. The drawing room had already been acquired by a museum, but the house was rebuilt and restored with uncommon care. Its steep roof, roof railing, fenestration and lack of wings and dependencies, as well as its material (wood), all mark it as foreign to the Southern styles of building.

Southern builders relied heavily on English, Dutch and Italian architectural guidebooks – details from Swan, Gibbs, Palladio and others are the rule – but The Lindens has an exterior composition far less sophisticated than these. Indeed, the proportions of the central bay would be thought astonishing and somewhat uncouth in Virginia. But it is an extremely interesting house and, moreover, superbly furnished. The floors of pine are stenciled in various designs along the borders and in the centers. What the lone pair of engaged two-storey Corinthian columns by the doorway lack in the way of fitness and harmoniousness with the rather provincial façade, they atone for in novelty and freedom from academic expectations. A front window blithely interrupts the main cornice and the somewhat pinched pediment carries a rather ill-proportioned window almost at its apex. One can almost feel the delight of the New England builder, fired with zeal and quite undismayed by the lack of a sensitive architect, and quite unbothered by the polish of Virginian façades.

On M Street there is a fine example of a 1770 two-storey brick town house, now used for shops, and on 28th Street stands a cottage built before 1775, remarkable for the width of its hewn weatherboarding.

Possibly the oldest house in the capital is now a museum known as the Old Stone House. The end walls rise two storeys in random fieldstone, but the end gables above them are filled in with brick. It was built in 1764 and later in that century was run as a tavern by one Cassandra Chew. In the 1780s she installed wooden paneling taken from another house to glorify her dining room, and also added a somewhat-too-handsome Adam mantel in an upstairs fireplace.

This sort of house, rude, honest and full of charm, must have been common in the eighteenth century. It would have suited those who wanted a good sturdy comfortable place but who had not the means, or perhaps not the inclination, for grander architectural exercises. No money has been spent here on carefully fired brick laid in Flemish bond, nor on moulded water tables or elegant chimneys or cut-stone entrances, yet inside it is sunny and snug and one would gladly sample a toddy at its hearth on any cold day.

Unlike the Massachusetts house, and quite unlike the Virginia and

28 Possibly the oldest house in the capital the Old Stone House has a charm of its own. The end walls are of random fieldstone, but the gables above are filled in with brick.

Maryland mansions of the period, the rough stone house does not even permit itself a pair of delicately detailed dormers on the third floor. Like everything else in the house the dormers are serviceable and pleasant to look at but without the least effort at luxury or show. It is all the more delightful to come across the paneling of the dining room and the bedroom mantel so lovingly installed by Mrs Chew. These features suggest what all architectural evidence indeed shows, that the instant an eighteenth-century American could possibly manage it, his or her thoughts turned to paneled drawing rooms and houses just like the ones in the architectural books. Or as near as never mind.

29 A sturdy, somewhat rude mid-eighteenth century dwelling, the Old Stone House still stands on M Street. Paneling of the second-floor dining room is believed to have come from another house of the period. It was installed about 1780.

30, 31 A rich colonial merchant built his house in Danvers, Massachusetts, in the 1750s. It was about to be destroyed when the present owner bought it in 1934 and moved it board by board to Washington where it now stands. The entrance hall of the rebuilt and lovingly restored house, now called The Lindens, was further embellished in the nineteenth century with romantic wallpaper from Paris by Dufour, showing Calypso's island and other dreamlike Arcadias.

32, 33 Two important old houses of the capital are The Lindens (*above*), which is an eighteenth-century Massachusetts house, and Dumbarton House (*right*), a more typically local style of mansion, built at the very end of the eighteenth century and moved from its original Georgetown site to another in the same neighborhood. The Massachusetts mansion of wood is an early northern essay at the grand manner; the other is a more conventional and academic (and perhaps more relaxed and confident) example. The Lindens is among the largest wooden houses built in the Colonies, and its interior trim and furnishings are of very high quality. Dumbarton House is now owned by the National Society of Colonial Dames, serving as national headquarters for that patriotic and social organization of descendants of leading colonial figures. It is handsomely furnished and is open to the public as a museum.

34, 35, 36 The most important house of the capital, the White House, was not completed during George Washington's presidency but has been occupied by all presidents since. The entrance lobby leads to a cross hall from which reception rooms open (*left*). The lobby, looking towards the north entrance door (*above*) adapts Roman decorative elements; the Red Room (*right*) opening from the cross hall contains some of the most important furniture of the early nineteenth century.

37 The White House has its main entrance on the north protected by a pedimented portico. Visiting dignitaries are met at the top of the steps by the president and his wife and escorted into the entrance lobby.

38 Mrs Ronald Reagan, wife of the president, stands in the Red Room, one of a suite thrown open for parties, and seen by tourists on guided tours.

39 It is doubtful whether the new republic could have held together without the personal leadership of George Washington, who was soon the subject of endless domestic bibelots across the country, such as this clock in the White House itself.

40, 41 White House wallpaper (*left*) reflects early American pride in harbors and ships, as at Boston. Classical acanthus leaves and dentils ornament a Palladian window treatment at the White House (*right*) lighter in effect, with its narrow muntins, than the earlier more robust treatments of colonial Maryland and Virginia.

42, 43 The Green Room (*left*) and the Blue Room (*below*) of the White House are additional reception rooms. The Green Room has traditionally been green, but of different tints; women complained that the green of President Jackson's regime was highly unflattering to their complexions. Beside the fireplace are two Sheffield-plate Argand lamps with oval mirror backs, each standing on a remarkably ingenious work table. In the Blue Room (*below*) are some of the gilt chairs made for President Monroe by the Parisian cabinetmaker Bellangé. The lighted portrait through the door is of Benjamin Franklin.

The Early Years of the Capital

If the Virginia and Maryland mansions of the eighteenth century were not utterly opulent, it was only because the means of making them so were not always at hand, and not for any lack of will on the part of the builders. But by contrast the style of the early nineteenth century aimed not at opulence so much as at elegance, or what was deemed "chaste"; and since critics commonly are a bit puritanical, through the innate defect of being critics rather than artists, this new "clean" style has been a particular enthusiasm of theirs.

It is not quite true to say that a new refinement and delicacy were embraced, but rather that an earlier exuberance was spurned, and a general paring down was everywhere detectable. Bricks were smaller, mortar joints thinner, though still laid in Flemish bond (without the festive glazed headers of 1740). Entrances were smart, one might say sleek, rather than monumental, and all openings, whether doors or windows, were sliced with a sharper knife, as it were. Wooden divisions separating window glass were lightened and thinned, producing a pleasing lightness in the façade, as well as a better view from indoors. No longer were rooms paneled floor to ceiling in walnut, with every moulding known to man plus a few others, but instead the new or Federal style abandoned full entablatures, and showed such a low regard for cornices that the plaster walls often met the plaster ceilings as naked as the day the trowel left them.

Stairways now exhibited a Spartan plainness. Newel posts were circular, turned neatly but plainly, without carving or embellishment. Handrails did not sweep round in full baroque curves; stair flights were usually straight; brackets beneath the individual treads were plain or, sometimes, lacking; spandrels were only rarely paneled and commonly had no decorative treatment of any kind.

But, as always, sensitive builders using judgment and skill saved such houses from becoming a series of plaster shoeboxes by indulging in a fanlight here, a recessed panel there, a little curve of a railing, or a discreet touch of delicate ironwork yonder. It says something for their sense of scale, their good workmanship and their eye for proportion that some of these houses are totally satisfying, not only to live in but also to look at.

45, 46, 47 The morning room at Arlington House (*left*) was built in the second spurt of construction activity in 1804. George Washington Parke Custis painted the heroic *Battle of Monmouth* on the right. The young woman of the easel portrait is Mildred Lee, daughter of General and Mrs Lee. Tudor Place (*below*) was built over a period of years before 1815. The portico which seems semicircular completes its circle inside the house by a semicircle of three floor-length windows. The view (*right*) is through the hall to the living room.

Two important examples, that are not at all typical of Federal style in Washington yet may be mentioned first, are Arlington House and Tudor Place, both of them built by grandchildren of Martha Washington by her first marriage to Colonel Daniel Parke Custis. These grandchildren were raised, following their father's death, at Mount Vernon and adopted by George Washington, though he left his own estate to a male Washington relative.

Arlington House is the work of architect George Hadfield. He and his sister Maria were of English parents and had grown up in Italy. Maria married a well-known London miniature painter, Richard Cosway. She met Thomas Jefferson in Paris, when he was the American minister there, and the two of them formed an emotional attachment, the dimensions of which are not yet fully known. Jefferson wrote her a last, and quite charming, letter not long before his death in 1826, by which time she was living in an Italian convent and was much concerned with education of the young, just as Jefferson was absorbed with his new love, the University of Virginia which he had founded.

Jefferson found in Maria's brother, George Hadfield, an architect of excellent soundness; that is, Hadfield agreed with him on important architectural matters such as Doric entablatures. Jefferson arranged for him to come to Washington to continue the supervision of the Capitol, and while there Hadfield undertook some outside work as well, including Arlington House.

Arlington is notable for its temple portico of overscaled brick columns plastered over. There had been various temple-portico buildings in America since the mid-eighteenth century, notably Redwood Library (1749), Whitehall, with its Corinthian portico (1765), as well as those Palladian porticoes of superimposed columns at Drayton Hall (1738) and Shirley (1765).

The first wing of Arlington House was completed in 1804, though the house was not finished until 1817, when the 140-foot-long façade greatly pleased citizens of Washington (as it still does) viewing it on its heights across the Potomac from the city. The builder, Washington Custis, was not only the adopted child of George Washington but also the future father-in-law of Robert E. Lee, chief hero of the Southern states in the Civil War. (Just the mention of his horse – a splendid beast named Traveller – brings a little surge of emotion to Southerners to this very day.) Lee loved Arlington better than any other house; he had visited it as a boy, so knew it even before his marriage there in 1831. It was from this dwelling that he departed to lead the Southern forces, never to return again. A particularly magnificent Himalayan cedar, possibly planted by Lee himself as a young lad, still stands at the back of the house.

There is the usual Southern hallway running the entire depth of the house, with rooms at each side. The main drawing room, however, the White Parlor, was used as a storage room for forty years until finally

48 A corner of Tudor Place reflects the elegance of its proportions and furnishings. A descendant of the original builders – Mr Thomas Peter and his wife Martha, the granddaughter of Martha Washington – still lives in the house today.

time and means to take it in hand resulted in General Lee's furnishing it in 1855. He himself is believed to have chosen the Victorian marble mantels and Victorian furniture, all of which is regarded by Southerners as virtually sacrosanct since it was Lee's, however deplorable it may seem to those who expect the house to be furnished in the style of 1800. The house, like the national graveyard surrounding it, is now owned by the national government and open to all.

Tudor Place is quite different, polished where Arlington House is rough, and it must rank as one of the most engaging dwellings of the continent. It was designed by an amateur architect, Dr William Thornton, who also designed the Capitol. The property was purchased from the Lowndes family, who had already built the two wings; the main part was built in 1805 by Mr Thomas Peter and his wife Martha, who was the granddaughter of Martha Washington. After an unbroken chain of family ownership, the house is still owned and lived in by their descendant, Mr Armistead Peter 3rd.

The south front certainly presents the more glamorous side with its large windows surmounted by arches, and its central temple forming a bow front of Tuscan columns, and – a highly original device – continuing the circle into the house's central hall, necessitating inverted bow windows. The north side, in the center of which is the front door, is, in Mr Peter's words, "as plain as a pikestaff." This side, at first glance, might be the entrance to an English rectory of the early nineteenth century. However, a longer look reveals a far more sophisticated façade, whose appeal rests on the fine proportions of the windows and door, and their relationship to the unadorned wall. To achieve this harmonious effect Thornton deliberately ignored the height of the rooms and the passages and staircase when he made the windows; if the ceilings did not go high enough for the windows, that was too bad, the windows would go through the ceiling. Such treatment was unnecessary on the south side where the rooms are lofty and of classic proportions, unencumbered by the "working" parts of the house such as staircases and passages, all of which are on the north side.

Another remarkable survivor, also designed by Dr Thornton, is Octagon House, now the national headquarters of American architects, who added a large new building at the back which did nothing to improve the looks of the garden, but which at least spared the elegant interiors of the old house the indignity of filing cabinets and clerks scampering about. It was named Octagon House presumably because it is not an octagon; it is not clear why it is such an odd shape. These things happen.

The house cost just twice what Thornton had estimated, which he may have found embarrassing, but then it is a nice house. It was built for John Tayloe who came from the splendid Virginia mansion, Mount Airy (1758), with its carved stone vases, arched loggia, stone quoins, and linking quadrants to the dependent buildings of the forecourt. How different the town house is from the country place.

The Tayloes entertained lavishly, and their house was as grand as any in town. With the War of 1812, Tayloe, being less than fully sympathetic to the Republicans, whose project this war was, moved his family to Mount Airy, and the house was lent to the French minister, though Tayloe himself remained as cavalry commander for the capital.

The White House was burned during that war and Tayloe then lent Octagon House to President Madison and his wife Dolley for a year. In a lovely upstairs room with curved walls pierced by elegant floor-length windows, Madison signed papers ending the war (the Treaty of Ghent).

One ghost of the house is said to be that of a Tayloe daughter, who flung herself off the staircase, a particularly lovely spiral one, in despair at star-crossed love; another is supposed to be that of a slave, who haunts underground passageways, now sealed up, while a third is that of Aaron Burr, the American traitor, who called here on Dolley Madison before setting sail in disgrace to England. The rooms and the furnishings of the house together provide a beautiful example of Federal taste and elegance, despite what any lively red-blooded architect of 1750 would consider an unwholesome and probably dangerous display of restraint.

Blair House is owned by the Federal Government, and used by visiting foreign dignitaries as home turf – the American president normally accompanies them to the front door to see them safely in, but does not himself enter.

The requirements of these visitors keep the staff from gathering moss. De Gaulle drank Evian water (not easy to find by the case in Washington, but it was found indeed) and needed his bed lengthened (which was done). The Arabian King Saud took a fancy to the library and announced he would sleep there (which he did with scimitared guards keeping watch) and his party managed to set a chair on fire with an incense-burner. Khrushchev disdained the state bedrooms and chose a small one on the third floor, usually occupied by lesser folk of an entourage, and had an aide who watched all food being prepared in the kitchen, and sampled it, too, before it was served to the boss (the aide never even fell ill from the Blair House food, either). Another guest, U Nu, had a room purified and set up a Buddhist altar in it – nothing whatever caught fire.

For all that, it is a quintessentially American house. Built in 1824 by a surgeon, it was bought in 1836 for $6,500 – it would cost somewhat more now – by Francis Preston Blair, a Kentucky man who was one of Andrew Jackson's unofficial advisers. He started up a newspaper, flourished, and when a daughter of the house married Samuel Phillips Lee, a cousin of Robert E. Lee, a house was built for her adjoining the Blair House, and the two buildings, now connected by doors cut through here and there, make up the existing structure. Officially it is called the President's Guest

House, but nobody, except possibly a government accountant somewhere, has ever called it anything but Blair House.

Historically, one of the crucial moments of the country's history occurred in the little study off the entrance hall, where Robert E. Lee was offered command of the Union armies in April 1861. He declined, of course, and became the hero of the Confederacy, a sort of King Arthur, Charlemagne and St John all in one.

Bacon House is not only one of the most important houses of the capital, but also one of the best examples of a house that is quite impossible to assign to a particular period. It was built in 1825, perhaps begun earlier. The land was owned in 1800 by Davy Burns, deeded in 1802 to William Dorsey who the same year conveyed it to John Tayloe, later to Jacob Wagner and in 1815 to Tobias Lear, who had been George Washington's secretary. Mr Lear is said to have been found dead with a bullet wound in the head in the garden of a small dwelling on this property. His widow sold the land to the US marshal in 1824 and the big brick house was built the following year.

Chief Justice John Marshall and Associate Justice Joseph Story lodged here during two winters (1831–33) when the Supreme Court was in session. Marshall was rather annoyed at having to move from his old accommodation. He noted, in a letter, the "revolutionary spirit" among the justices

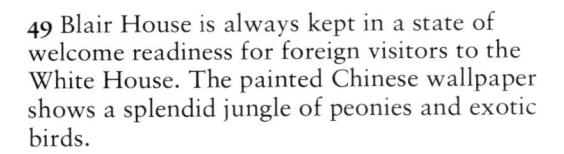

49 Blair House is always kept in a state of welcome readiness for foreign visitors to the White House. The painted Chinese wallpaper shows a splendid jungle of peonies and exotic birds.

(that is, the decision to quit the old boarding house) and he expected it would, "like most other revolutions, work inconvenience and mischief in its progress."

All the same, this orphan of the revolution moved with Mr Story to Bacon House, as it is now known, and was quite content there until obliged to move again in 1833, when he recommenced his alarms: "What is to become of us? What arrangement can be made?" But of course arrangements were made. The justices had still to leave their families behind, however, since life in the new capital was a hardship on wives and children, and indeed many early civil servants kept bachelor hall in Washington.

The house was bought in 1836 by Governor Spriggs of Maryland for his daughter, who was married to William Thomas Carroll, clerk of the Supreme Court. For sixty years the place was called Carroll House. It was said Mrs Carroll kept two sets of servants, one for day and one for night, because she entertained on such a vast scale. She lived to an advanced age and to the last received her guests standing.

In 1896 the house was bought by Chief Justice Melville Fuller, who took particular pleasure in holding court conferences in the house where Chief Justice Marshall had done the same some sixty-five years earlier. After Fuller's death, the house was sold in 1911 to a sister of Henry Thaw's, who had married and divorced the Earl of Yarmouth. Various tenants then came and went, including Senator Medill McCormick. Representative Robert Low Bacon rented it in 1923, bought it in 1925, and it has been Bacon House ever since.

From the street you may suppose the entrance bay, which has a strong Federal or Regency look, to be original. It was, however, added by Chief Justice Fuller after 1896. He also added the glassed-in room called the gallery. The Countess of Yarmouth, though in brief possession of the house, must have been quite busy with it. The handsome black marble mantels and chandeliers – so appropriate for the house – are from her occupancy.

Virginia Murray Bacon, widow of the celebrated representative from New York, was a leading grande dame of the capital. The portrait of her in the dining room was painted when she was four. It was tedious to stand still for it, she observed in her old age, but the older she got, the more closely she resembled the little girl in the portrait. Sometimes she received guests at the extreme end of the drawing room. They could therefore look down the long axis of the public rooms from the portrait to the aged hostess and remark on the likeness, an observation that did not by any means displease her.

She kept a good many candles going, which possibly discolored the walls a little, but the effect in the drawing room was impressive when reflected in the great rococo mirror of which Mrs Bacon was so fond. It is

50 The straight, plain lines of the staircase in this Georgetown house are typical of the Federal period.

carved with a curly-tailed dog and a pointer, to say nothing of a stag, a boar, a cow, some elm tree branches, a squirrel, a phoenix, a flute, a clarion, a natural trumpet, and a good many other creatures, all much admired by Mrs Bacon, who was not above saying that this or that animal reminded her of some particular person.

She was a Republican, but lost no time meeting Democrats, or indeed anybody who was either powerful or agreeable; hence she had one of the largest circles ever known to Washington. In her old age she sometimes rested her eyes during a concert; but she not only liked the arts herself but felt she should be present whenever they were performed or displayed. She investigated minutely every new style of painting, getting round on a stick, if her legs failed her. On one occasion she was reduced to viewing an exhibition from a wheelchair, but having acquired some posters of the exhibits rolled up in mailing tubes she stuck these out of the sides of her chair, and passed triumphantly through the crowd as if in a Scythian chariot.

But back to the house: like many another house of the capital, it is perfectly possible, given a little effort, to determine when the mantels, chandeliers, cove ceilings, two-storey bays and so on were added. But often there is no way to tell just by looking. The huge portrait of the fourth Earl of Dunmore, one of Virginia Bacon's predecessors, who was the last royal governor of Virginia, is not original with the house: it is a copy of a Reynolds portrait that Mrs Bacon saw at the National Gallery in 1976.

The house is full of mementoes, pictures of President and Mrs Eisenhower and dozens of others, and of bibelots that had some particular meaning to the Bacons. In any book on houses it could fall into a number of categories, and while "Federal" is not quite right, neither is any other. Mrs Bacon, like other sensible strong-minded householders, took what she found and added what she missed, without concerning herself overmuch with architectural or decorating styles.

She was the nautilus, after all, and the old house merely her shell, however chambered or pearly or even, in some lights on some evenings, adamantine. At her death she left it to a foundation to preserve, not as a museum, but as a meeting place for statesmen and (in case statesmen sounded too grand) others devoting their lives to civic service, to exchange views on world problems.

The curator, Mr Lawrence Kolp, has observed that one aspect of the house not revealed by the masonry is the abiding presence of dogs. "In the past six decades, at least, there have always been good dogs here. Appropriate, strong, willful, charming, maybe even cunning dogs. But dogs. Yes. Dogs. You know."

Indeed, there are living, or once-living, aspects to virtually every house in the capital that the visitor must supply from his imagination, his intuition, or perhaps his heart.

51, 52, 53 The Tuscan columns of the Arlington House portico are brick finished with stucco (*left*), here temporarily removed for repair work. The early nineteenth-century house was designed by George Hadfield, an Englishman encouraged by Jefferson to move to the capital to superintend ongoing construction of the Capitol. The house was built by a member of Martha Washington's family and later owned by Gen. Robert E. Lee, who furnished its drawing room with high Victorian furniture in the 1850s, though the trim of some of the rooms (*below right*) is decidedly Federal. The pediment supported by uncommonly heavy columns is an early example of the Classic Revival style launched by Jefferson, and soon to spread throughout the country.

54, 55 Tudor Place, an early nineteenth-century house built by a member of Martha Washington's family, boasts a circular Tuscan domed temple set into its façade (*left*), which continues into its main hall (*below*). The window sashes open to give access to the lawn. The panes are uncommonly large, the muntins slender and elegant.

56, 57, 58 The façade of Tudor Place opposite the temple front is determinedly plain (*left*) and chaste. The house, designed by William Thornton, is brick with yellow stucco and is considered one of the finest of the East Coast. The paneled door is set in a recessed and paneled archway with delicate fanlight; though simple, the details are handled with great refinement. The interior is equally polished and less plain, with Adam, Chippendale and Federal touches, beautiful carpets and porcelains.

59, 60, 61 Octagon House was the town house of a great Virginia plantation family and was lent to President Madison after the White House was burned in the War of 1812. Designed by William Thornton, its construction was followed carefully by George Washington who frequently rode over to see it. The reason for its unusual shape, more nearly hexagonal than octagonal, is unknown, but its curved bay and little Ionic entrance portico were as greatly admired in 1800 as today. The treaty ending the war was signed in 1815 in this circular upstairs room (*below right*).

62, 63 The stairways of Octagon House illustrate the new taste of 1800 for republican simplicity and lack of ostentation. The balusters are as plain as a lumber yard can make them, and the brackets are simply scrolled, without carving; there is no paneled dado, and the flights are not emphasized but flow gently together in one continuous three-storey run. Graceful and light in weight, they are delicate and unobtrusive.

64 Blair House (*above*) is used by foreign dignitaries visiting the president. Situated just across Pennsylvania Avenue from the White House, it consists of two nineteenth-century houses of the Blair and Lee families, now thrown into one. The enriched cornice and delicately garlanded mantelpiece contrast with the less patrician ornaments.

65 The dining room (*right*) of The Octagon, or Octagon House, gives no hint that the mansion fell on hard times and was in a sorry state, occupied by poor renters, when it was taken over in the present century by the American Institute of Architects. It is now elegantly restored and open to the public.

66, 67 Bedrooms of Blair House (*below and right*) show the increasing heaviness of effect in American taste after 1825, presaging the ponderous Victorian style to come. The house is strongly identified with President Jackson and later with Gen. Robert E. Lee.

68 The Marine Commandant's House (*right*) of the early nineteenth century has an unusual vaulted ceiling and a staircase retaining the paneled dado along its flights, but also the simple newel post that would have seemed overly plain and unfinished in a colonial mansion of the South. It is always shipshape, some say the cleanest house in the capital, and provides a beautiful softly lighted setting for receptions at the Evening Parades.

69, 70, 71 Decatur House (*left*) was built by Commodore Stephen Decatur with money from his victories over the Barbary Pirates, and Benjamin Latrobe designed a beautiful Federal house for him on Lafayette Square in front of the White House. Decatur was killed in a duel in 1820; his widow moved to a smaller place and the house was subsequently occupied by French, Russian and British ministers, two secretaries of state and various other notables. Now a National Trust property, it is a museum. The figure (*below left*) is one of a pair supporting the candelabra on the mantel. Bacon House (*right*) was long called Marshall House since Chief Justice John Marshall lodged there in the 1830s. Later, another chief justice owned it, and at last the Bacon family. For decades this dining room has been a center of social and political life in the capital, and it will now become a foundation center for discussions in the field of public affairs. The portrait is of the late Virginia Murray Bacon at the age of four. Before her death in her 80s she was one of the capital's leading society figures.

72, 73, 74, 75 Bacon House, a late Federal mansion identified with Chief Justice Marshall who boarded there in the 1830s, has a homey look despite its size and long history as setting for some of the most prestigious entertaining in the capital. Its door is covered with ivy, and its incidental tables loaded with photographs of the great. The late nineteenth-century stair is reached through a very non-Federal door with a leaded-glass top.

76, 77, 78 Bacon House (*left*) was long a scene of entertaining in which countless guests somehow managed to fit easily among the furniture and bric-à-brac. The chief reception rooms (*below right*) were candle-lit, warm and crowded. A former owner, a Countess of Yarmouth, added the chandeliers in this century. The gallery (*top right*), a room also added in this century, is packed with mementoes, and was the setting for many quiet conversations and informal gatherings.

The Victorian City

The time has arrived when the expansiveness and exuberance of the Victorian era are no longer thoroughly despised, and "gimcrack" is no longer the only adjective to describe the marvelous splendors of the nineteenth century.

There are more Victorian houses in Washington than anybody realizes, partly because heroic efforts were made earlier this century to turn Victorian dwellings into Late Georgian monuments, or into snug chintz-covered informal country lodges. It was an article of faith, both in Washington and in America generally, that all the best people had dark Georgian six-paneled entrance doors with small brass knockers, and while it was a plain fact that Georgetown, for example, was composed chiefly of Victorian dwellings, still it was thought to be an embarrassing fact that should be minimized or concealed whenever possible.

Many a Victorian window opening was altered, many a vast Victorian roof with mad dormers was lowered, and many a Victorian gallery or porch was quietly ripped off in the effort (sometimes naive, sometimes barbarous, and only occasionally successful) to make a high Victorian structure accord more closely with the Georgian or Federal legacy. Some Victorian houses resisted these cosmetic operations with the determination of an elephant.

As early as the late nineteenth century a little cult began to flourish in favor of eighteenth-century American houses. Thus the Victorian style began to be looked down on while still in its heyday. Such influential architectural firms as McKim, Mead and White essayed Colonial details here and there, rather in the manner of someone attaching the most charming features of the gazelle to a somewhat astonished wart-hog. There was also the great impetus of Williamsburg, the eighteenth-century capital of Virginia, which was restored in our own century. The quality of the workmanship there, the beauty of the brickwork and the elegance of the design, had a wide effect on American taste, highly detrimental to the Victorian dream, or nightmare, as the new chaste purists called it.

It remained for a new wave of concrete slabs, gypsum board, plywood, and the total repudiation of ornament and all personal eccentricity, to effect a change of taste once again, and this time more favorable to Victorian splendor. There is, after all, nothing quite so effective as a few

79 The Turkish Embassy began life in 1914 as town house for a millionaire who patented fluted bottle tops for soft drinks and was known as the bottle-top king. His architect was George Oakley Totten Jr., one of the pre-eminent purveyors of the Beaux Arts style of mansion building to the capital. The glass porte cochère is one of the few remaining intact.

80, 81 Frederick Douglass, one of the most celebrated black citizens of the post Civil War capital, came to the city in 1871, edited a newspaper, served as marshal and as recorder of deeds, and became minister to Haiti in 1889. He was among the first to demand the enfranchisement of the nation's blacks, although a vote on this question in the capital in 1866 showed only 35 white citizens in favor of it. Douglass had a town house, now the Museum of African Art, and a suburban villa (*left and above*) called Cedar Hill. It has a sunny, homey, unpretentious air, and is maintained as a museum. To many citizens it is virtually a shrine.

miles of concrete and glass to stir the dark latent instincts, long suppressed, for the wedding-cake effect.

Sometimes, Victorian shades into Greek Revival, sometimes into French and Italian Renaissance, sometimes into a hint of Frank Lloyd Wright. Indeed, a touchstone of Victorian architecture is its propensity to veer off in some amazing direction or other. And yet houses of the period have virtues, once taken for granted and therefore ignored, but now properly honored. Few were shoddily constructed. Everything, from the cornices to the eaves brackets to the tile fireplaces to the interior shutters, was worked with care and with a skill no longer expected in modern houses. Ceilings were high, porches were spacious.

An interesting house – occupied by Frederick Douglass from the 1870s to the 1890s – is to be seen in the Anacostia section of the capital. This is a poor and almost entirely black quarter, but when the Douglass house was built it was rural. The wide porch, with classic columns of modest height and modest effect, could be part of a farmhouse in Mississippi or Indiana. There is no attempt to impress anybody.

Douglass was born a slave, and rose to become a minister to Haiti. He was one of America's first black heroes, and his house reflects both his consciousness of his stature and importance (do not overlook the un-expected eighteenth-century Chippendale chairs) and his unwillingness to give himself airs. Apparently he was a very human fellow. It is said he had a little study into which no woman entered unless she gave him a kiss. His rhetoric – he was an admired orator – did much to waken support for the cause of American blacks.

Instead of lavish cornices, he used wallpaper to achieve the dignity he desired at the point the wall meets the ceiling. A modest kerosene lamp lights a dressing table. One feels he would have chosen mules rather than pastoral sheep to graze beneath his trees. (This may be the place to observe the astonishing affection in which mules are held by the best elements of American society, possibly because mules have a more impressive gravity, intelligence and natural sweetness than horses.) He could not resist an excessively carved chair, one is sorry to notice, but few men can escape the particular grossness of the age into which they are born. Still, the house has an interesting air of sobriety and seriousness.

Beyond doubt the great Victorian house remaining in Washington is the Christian Heurich mansion, built in the 1890s. Mr Heurich was a brewer of beer and had other German virtues, none of them giddy or light. He had a disastrous fire in his brewery in the 1880s, a circumstance that led to his capping all the chimneys of his later mansion, lest anybody should be tempted to do anything frivolous with the fireplaces, such as light a fire in them.

His house, incredibly enough, is of concrete. It is merely veneered with brown sandstone. At a basement entrance to the side, you can peer up to

82 Very little has changed in the Heurich Mansion, now owned by the Columbia Historical Society, who have opened it to the public.

the concrete structural wall. Few rooms are as small as eighteen by eighteen feet. Beneath the floors he stuffed asbestos. In all directions he overbuilt. Repairmen are astonished to find three steel I-beams together, presumably in case two should collapse for some reason. The plaster hangs on metal lath.

There is some good Art Nouveau metalwork. Most of the furniture, surprisingly, was made down the road by German-American craftsmen, and it is not to be trifled with. All lights are fitted for both gas and electricity (as in the Vanderbilt mansion in Newport). The bathtub is ornamented outside with colored swags and garlands. The study is decorated with portrait medallions reflecting the owner's taste in historians. The house is dark, and the dark walls of the great stair hall are ornamented with applied metal decorations in silver leaf.

It is the only house remaining intact that was built by a Washington man engaged in purely local business, not government, who lived and died involved in the concerns of a town rather than a nation.

The house is wonderfully solid, wonderfully confident, and wonderfully touching in its assurance that here civilization has come into ultimate flower. It is a spectacular piece of good fortune that it is now owned (and opened) by the Columbia Historical Society. Few houses anywhere that are less than a century old so vividly convey the remote past. Visitors gaze at it as if it were a Saxon cairn or a Druid temple or some other monument of a past too distant to be recognizable.

No house has a stronger Victorian feeling than the Toutorskys', and few houses give so clear an idea of the heights Victorian taste might reach. One is hard pressed to say how the decor came to be so beautiful; few people need to be reminded that the average family should not be turned loose with an unlimited quantity of ebony and ormolu and rich fabrics and carved doors, and vast black pianos and sofas with gilded mounts, to say nothing of a leopard rug, stuffed armadillo and lion, and plenty of gleaming old icons plus a gold harp. The Toutorskys have all this and more. Here is God's plenty. If one were weaned, so to speak, on bleached Scandinavian driftwood or three Japanese twigs in a jug, then the shock of the Toutorsky style might prove fatal, or possibly therapeutic.

One may well tremble to think of the difficulty of transforming a mélange of stuffed lions and numinous icons into a setting that is neither absurd nor mad, but gorgeous. The rich deep colors, the limited light gleaming on polished wood, the contrasting textures of fur and metal, all have something to do with it, no doubt, but the result is a magic one cannot readily believe. Just as at Chartres one may be shocked at this detail or that, yet awed by the vaulting synthesis, so one is rather lost in the Toutorsky richness. Music is a family passion, and it is translated into their surroundings, which have a contrapuntal and baroque harmony that one may rejoice to comprehend, but would perhaps be a fool to try to imitate.

83 For years the American vice president had no official house, but now the present incumbent presumably enjoys sunny afternoons on this porch of what formerly was the house of the chief of naval operations. It was designated as home for the vice president in the Nixon Administration. Although there are guards at the gate, the long driveway makes them invisible from the house, which has an air of the countryside about it, and quite a pretty little garden stuffed with homey flowers.

Washington is a Victorian city visually, and it will be recalled that in the decade of Victoria's accession to the throne the American chief justice was still muttering about the succession of boarding houses in which he was obliged to live, simply because the capital was still a little town and there were not enough houses to go around. It was only later, during the Victorian heyday, that the place began to look like a city. There are today neglected (neglected, that is, by those who orchestrate common applause) Victorian monuments such as St Mark's church, in which structural steel is used for aesthetic effect as well as for such trifling purposes as holding up the roof. But apart from monuments, there are engaging Victorian façades all over the town. I myself once lived up in the fourth-floor dome of a now-demolished Victorian mansion, and can testify to the solidity of the structure. The dome was copper, sheathed with red tiles, and when this crowning feature finally heated up in June it stayed hot till Thanksgiving and not a degree of Centigrade or even Fahrenheit was thoughtlessly wasted to the outside air during this entire period.

On some nights there were parties to which, needless to say, an American country lad was not invited, but from which he might derive joy all the same. I once encountered a majestic old lady dragging an eight-foot silk train up the steps, and wearing egret feathers (illegal since 1910, I believe) in her hair. All this in the 1940s. I do not think such people would have entered, or such substantial majesty have flourished, if the place were glass and concrete.

Once you tear down a Victorian mansion of this stature, the egret feathers all disappear and while we all know that is good (the egret must and shall be protected) still we all know that is bad, too. For architecture does, in spite of us, exert a fierce pressure on how we live, even on how we walk and dress. I would not nowadays dream of wearing diamonds and egret feathers to supper. And yet one may walk contentedly – with a sharp eye for approaching muggers, of course – through block after block of Victorian houses, some boasting turrets, some festive with Italian Villa Revival towers, some with yawning entrance arches like caves, and some with prim rosettes of moulded brick.

We come now, in this sweeping survey of our Washington dwellings, to what that particular Mrs Malaprop from Mississippi would have called the very height of the epitome. For here we deal with the Beaux Arts houses of Washington, more beau than artful, possibly, but a wonder to all when they were built and an even greater wonder now. Many began life as a tycoon's toy, but today are embassies.

Unlike modern man, modern nations have not yet lost that desire to impress the common folk. The Cameroons hold forth in a Loire-château-type bastion, while the French dazzle all, descending their Jacobean staircase, and the Indonesians rest contentedly behind carved marble vases and columns of rare Italian marble, rightly proud of the most gorgeous Art Nouveau entrance hall this side of Brussels.

The Italians are somewhat Tudor and the Japanese are Regency, or were until they built a new place that looks, of all things, Japanese. The Turks favor Roman Renaissance; the Spanish prefer Venetian Renaissance; the Mexicans adhere to English Palladian, and the Belgians naturally veer to the Parisian grand manner; the Peruvians hold to English Georgian. The Swedish embassy reflects that country's love of the Mediterranean, and the Germans and the Swiss reveal their national enthusiasm for the wholesome life by living in houses that suggest gymnasia.

Only the British, one is obliged to say, have shown a singular lack of imagination. They live in a British neo-Palladian mansion designed by a singularly British architect, the late Sir Edwin Lutyens, and might as well never have left Surrey, in a sense. It would have cost no more – probably less – if they had built in a breezy Polynesian manner with palm-thatched roofs. It is not really the expected thing, in this capital, for a nation to choose its own national style for its embassy. It is thought a bit chauvinistic.

Chauvinistic or not, there the British Embassy is, unabashedly English and complete with a garden growing some of the best roses in Washington. The lovely old climber, 'Gloire de Dijon' (a French rose introduced in 1853), was recently added to the garden, probably to mark the inexorable advance of Progress and Britain's forward-looking involvement with the European Community. In any case, the folk of Washington admire it vastly, and charity benefits held there draw great crowds. The British have an unfair advantage over most Washington embassies, in that they speak English well, for the most part, and have read many of the same books Americans have, in school. This is by no means true of the French, say, who read only Edgar Allan Poe, and who all wish to view the Grand Canyon and see Indians.

The great double staircases of the British Embassy, with heroic-sized portraits of British monarchs gazing down, give every visitor a sense of stateliness, even if one has only come in hopes of a cup of tea and a free strawberry (if it is the Queen's Birthday).

There used to be a large and magnificent bronze by Henry Moore in the garden, on loan. A member of the Royal Family is said to have observed on a visit here that it resembled a particularly sad example of back trouble. But then art so often does. Tucked away somewhere are a little Japanese garden with a stone lantern, and a swimming pool, shaded by trees and beastly cold to American hides, but very beautiful. The Prince of Wales is believed to have swum naked in it. Once there was also an embassy cat with a stump tail, said to have been abbreviated by a lawn mower. It used to patrol beneath the table during formal dinners, and though ritually shooed out on great occasions, always managed to get back in. Its fame was such that newspapers took note of its passing.

84 Ivy seems to ramble at will over the brick façade of the Toutorsky mansion.

The British Embassy has always set a good table, according to those who have dined there, though the cuisine is said to be not always, or even usually, what one thinks of as the British national fare. At a party given for Queen Elizabeth the embassy was decked with crimson roses, and candles out in the garden. President Ford arrived early, before the Queen, and had to be asked to drive around the block until radioed of the arrival of his hostess. A lone bagpipe played slow haunting tunes towards midnight and people cried and said it was the most beautiful official party they ever went to or ever heard of. The cat behaved fairly well.

A visitor should not miss, by the way, the quite handsome pavement of slates laid on edge beneath the stone garden-front portico, a familiar element of the Lutyens style that has proved surprisingly durable.

The Turkish Embassy at Sheridan Circle (Sheridan Circle is the center of the great collection of magnificent Washington houses) was built in 1914 for a millionaire who, among other important contributions to the republic, had invented crimped metal tops for soda-pop bottles, and been handsomely rewarded for it. His wife was a soprano and in the early twenties the couple often entertained with musical evenings. In the thirties the house was sold to the Turkish government.

One of Washington's grandes dames, Mrs John B. Henderson, the wife of a senator, had a house on Sixteenth Street which became a great center for Washington social life. Mrs Henderson was an immensely interesting woman, even by Washington standards, but the particular bee in her bonnet was her determination to make Sixteenth Street the only street of consequence in the capital. Had she not built her own mansion on it? Then what, pray, was everybody waiting for? She made the Congress (not to split hairs about it) designate her street The Avenue of the Presidents in 1913, and took off for a well-earned vacation abroad, for she had put a great deal of time and energy into forcing the Congress to her will. Scarcely was she out of town, however, than the sheepish Congress changed the name back to Sixteenth Street. Everyone in Washington knew they would never have dared such a spineless reversal if Mrs Henderson were in residence. Never mind. Mrs Henderson, not to be outmaneuvered, bought up Sixteenth Street property and put the heat on, socially and politically, selecting targets whom she deemed suitable as neighbors.

One of her failures was the millionaire who built the house now occupied by the Turkish ambassador. Mrs Henderson had introduced that man to his lovely soprano wife at her own house and, furthermore, she had carefully explained to him the endless merits of Sixteenth Street. But such is the coarseness and ingratitude of the American male that this man deliberately built his great mansion at Sheridan Circle. As Mrs Henderson must have frequently pointed out, he could have been her neighbor. At least his house was not an embassy. Mrs Henderson was especially anxious that all embassies be on her street. She died before the Turks bought the

85 Beaux Arts houses like this one are still a source of surprise and wonder.

Sheridan Circle house for their embassy. They had considered – and rejected – a Sixteenth Street site.

The world, or at least the glittering world of Washington, was moving away from Mrs Henderson, and her Avenue of the Presidents. It is a mercy she did not live to see her old mansion torn down, and her majestical avenue come to be regarded as rather third-class. It was as if in London one had spent years establishing Mayfair, and then everybody perversely moved to Notting Hill.

Today, the acids of modernity have eaten even into Massachusetts Avenue. The Russians, Germans and Japanese have built elsewhere, although Massachusetts remains preeminent for majestic embassies. These mansions, most of them built before the First World War, are rather costly (ruinously so, some might say) to maintain. One of them, the Argyle Guest House, now accepts paying guests. Built in 1901 for a millionaire, who moved to Washington because it was clear to him that it was (or soon would be) the most beautiful and cultivated city of America, it boasted the first garage for automobiles in town.

The man had a naval background, as may be guessed by the shells and tridents worked in here and there. The builder chose freely from his various inspirations: the entrance is strongly suggestive of the Italian Renaissance, the marvelous twin cylindrical towers remind one of the great French châteaux, and the central area of the roof is reminiscent of charming old houses in Ghent or Antwerp. The extremely large stone cat that perches on a parapet high above Massachusetts Avenue is harder to place. It is not quite Old Kingdom, and yet it is not quite Gothic gargoyle, either. (It was erected as a kind of memorial after the owner's beloved cat died.) The lintels over the windows are assertively mid-Georgian. It is all magnificent and funny in equal measure, and one would give much to live there; but, alas, one would need to give very much indeed to keep on living there. The bill merely for repairing the stone cat would be enough to give one pause.

The Mexican Embassy, of buff-colored brick instead of the usual limestone, granite and marble, is a mansion built in 1911 for Franklin MacVeagh, who was President Taft's Treasury Secretary. He is said to have had no idea the house was being built for him, until on Christmas Eve his wife took him to see it. He admired it, of course, and his wife gave it to him for a Christmas present. The housewarming doubled as a party honoring the Tafts' daughter, and all Washington turned out for the occasion.

It served as guest house for visiting British Prime Minister Balfour, as well as for the King and Queen of Belgium. The Mexican government bought it in 1921 but in deference to Secretary MacVeagh, who had so loved the place, they made no changes until after his death in 1934. Then they added the enormous mural that runs along the stair walls to the third floor. A thousand guests fit comfortably, or reasonably comfortably, in the second-floor reception rooms. The house has nine bathrooms, in case one wonders about such things in contemplating houses of this scale in Washington.

Virtually all mansions of this period in Washington have magnificently carved staircases, and wall treatments are elaborate, paneled sometimes, or covered with tooled leather or gold leaf, or tapestries, or paintings, or (as here) wainscoted with tiles (azulejos) in handsome designs.

Anderson House, now a museum and headquarters of a patriotic organization called the Society of the Cincinnati, was built in 1905 for an American diplomat, Larz Anderson. Sometimes private parties are held there, and it has been used by an American president to honor a visiting king at a great dinner. The expected lavishness prevails. More than a dozen marbles have been used for the interiors. One room, measuring thirty by eighty feet, has a lovely curved mezzanine of wrought iron supported by twisted Venetian columns, and at night the blaze of crystal and the gleaming floors of parquetry still remind the visitor that there are grander things than fluorescent tubes and wall-to-wall carpeting.

The Sulgrave Club, a smart place indeed though not abounding with the jet set, was built in 1901 for the millionaire Herbert Wadsworth, who had great agricultural interests in New York. Parties at this club are reassuringly decorous. Members like to dine quietly, and afterwards have their coffee on Empire sofas before fireplaces in which electric lights do their best to look like glowing coals. One has the impression of leading a civilized life after an evening spent within these walls.

The Cosmos Club, also on Massachusetts Avenue, now lets women walk right in the front door, bold as brass. From time to time somebody raises the vulgar question whether women should be admitted to membership, thus far with the expected male-membership answer. The walls boast photographs of roughly a thousand Nobel Prize winners who have at one time been members. The dining room is often full, and the place is celebrated for popovers as well as impressive brains. It was a quite handsome farmhouse of 1873 until in 1899 Richard Townsend, a president of the Erie and Pittsburgh Railroad, had it transformed into a reasonable adaptation of the Petit Trianon of Versailles, and one may look in vain for any rural touches. The house was inherited by Mrs Sumner Welles, wife of President Franklin Roosevelt's friend and Undersecretary of State. The president stayed here for three weeks before his inauguration in 1933.

The club had for decades been housed in Dolley Madison's old house on Lafayette Square. Mrs Madison, widow of the American president, fell on very hard times financially but was given an income by Congress (which was more than they did for Jefferson, who had to sell his important library for cash; it later became the nucleus of the Library of Congress). Mrs Madison ended her days happily as a grande dame of the capital, as was only right for a woman of her charm. The Cosmos Club maintained the dignity and brilliance of her old house before moving into its present mansion in 1952.

The great ballroom has magnificent arched mirrors trimmed in gold and an assortment of Cupids energetically supporting medallions in the fine cove ceiling, topped by the multicolored goddess Aurora bringing joy to the world at dawn. The lobby is of Caen stone with lavender marble columns and a white and green marble floor. It is both safe and sad to say that few houses will ever be built in Washington like this one.

The Belmont House, a gorgeous folly of 1909, was home to the then Prince of Wales during his visit to the capital in 1919. The builder was Perry Belmont, son of the New York financier and himself a former member of Congress and minister to Spain. His wife was a divorced woman, and the wedge-shaped mansion was called, rather unkindly, the Opening Wedge, on the theory that the Belmonts probably would use it to work their way into Washington society, divorce still being considered an obstacle to social advancement. However, the Belmonts had no trouble at all in attracting luminous guests.

The dining room's stone doorway is a stunning Venetian affair with carved shells, Cupids and eagles, and one almost expects the Doge's barge to pull up any minute. The mantels came from various palaces, the Japanese emperor contributed a painted screen, the lusters of the chandeliers are rock crystal and amethyst; it is little wonder the Belmonts failed to find a buyer in the Depression.

The International Order of the Eastern Star, a fraternal organization, acquired the great house in 1935 and has succeeded in preserving much of the Belmont splendor.

The Belgian Embassy was a private mansion built as late as 1931, the depths of the Depression, for Raymond Baker, who had been President Woodrow Wilson's director of the mint. There is no connection, of course, but one cannot help wondering. People called the site Baker's Acres, since it had thirteen of them in what is now one of the city's ultra-fashionable areas. The first Mrs Baker was heiress to a fortune deriving from a product said to be helpful in cases of headache, upset stomach and/or hangover. The second Mrs Baker was heiress to a Detroit automobile fortune. In 1940 a leading American hostess, Mrs Edward T. Stotesbury, leased the house from Baker's widow, whose first husband had been Mrs Stotesbury's son. Mrs Stotesbury entertained magnificently: half the power of the capital was at her house on the day the Japanese attacked Pearl Harbor. The party was for Alben Barkley, later the American vice president. An understandable anxiety prevailed.

Dumbarton Oaks is one of the greatest houses of Georgetown, and it is no more an example of a Beaux Arts effort than a battleship is. Still, in a sketch of Washington houses, it has to go somewhere. It was built in 1801 by William Dorsey, said to be one of the handsomest gentlemen who ever lived in this town. The early nineteenth-century orangery has an eighteenth-century look, which is fitting since the land itself, once a farm owned by Colonel Ninian Beall, was a famous Washington landmark (called Rock of Dumbarton), which appears on an important map of 1716.

Various important families have owned the house over the years. John C. Calhoun, the American vice president, bought it in 1822. It was transformed into a mid-Victorian fashion plate with a rather phallic tower and a new Mansard roof and a few other improvements. The gardens in the mid-nineteenth century were famous; the place was then called Monterrey. In 1920 it was bought by Robert Woods Bliss, a wealthy Foreign Service officer. He and his wife Mildred spent twenty years on the house, undoing all the Victorian improvements and transforming it into the present impressive mansion.

For years Mrs Bliss worked with Beatrix Farrand on the gardens, among the handsomest of the continent. A great hue and cry went up a few years ago when a pair of cedars, not especially magnificent ones, were threatened by the need for more working space – since the house is now used by Harvard University as a center for Byzantine and pre-Columbian scholars. The grading of the north vista of the garden would have been altered. Such was the clamor raised in Washington that the garden was left untouched.

The Blisses redid the interiors and added the great music room, in which Stravinsky, Paderewski, Landowska and other notable musicians have performed. The Dumbarton Oaks Conference, forecasting the establishment of the United Nations, was held in this room in 1944. During the

87 An owl carved in wood makes an attractive detail in this Sixteenth-Street house.

Second World War it was the scene of important discussions and decisions on research in atomic weaponry. The house now suggests the damn-what-it-costs approach of the Beaux Arts mansions of Washington, but of course Dumbarton Oaks trails more historical glory in its train than any of the others.

In the 1960s the architect Philip Johnson designed a museum for the scholarly center's important art collection. This building, widely admired for its own merit, is modestly set to one side with plenty of trees, so it does not jar with the style of the main mansion.

A Massachusetts Avenue mansion identified with a newspaper fortune is the Indonesian Embassy, which was built not by a publishing tycoon but by an Irishman, Thomas F. Walsh, who hit gold out West in 1896. He erected this sixty-room house in 1903. His daughter, Evalyn, married Edward Beale McLean, a member of the colorful and important family that owned *The Washington Post*. It was in this mansion that they arranged the purchase of the celebrated Hope Diamond. A remarkable feature of the house is its three-storey stair hall finished with a stained-glass roof. The columns of the open gallery of the second floor are Corinthian, but the stairs themselves rise and divide and sweep upward in a superb mahogany Art Nouveau exercise designed by John Andersen of New York.

One of the most colorful characters of the capital in her day was Alice Pike Barney, whose Studio House on Sheridan Circle is finished in stucco; although it would be thought a large house today (three storeys plus attic), it seems modest enough in comparison with the standard mansions of the neighborhood. But in contrast to these houses the larger windows opening onto the Circle have slanted sills, which was certainly not standard, and the little ones of Spanish design on the first floor – a quatrefoil super-imposed on a square – pivot out. This can hardly have seemed correct to those whose sills were flat, whose walls were marble, and whose windows went up and down, with none of this swinging in and out, like some Spanish windmill.

Mrs Barney was born rich and married a rich manufacturer of train cars. Her main dwelling was on R Street and this studio was her great toy. She painted – Whistler was one of her teachers and he warned her that she was terribly clever, but this did not stop her from being advanced and a trifle arty, as far as conservative citizens could tell. Not only did she paint (Shaw and Ruth St Denis sat for portraits) but she wrote plays and prodded Congress to establish the Sylvan Theater, where she directed them. She helped establish the Neighborhood Settlement House, which was a worthy thing, but she is especially remembered for her friendship with people like Djuna Barnes and Romaine Brooks, and for her elaborate parties and tableaux at Studio House. She loved rich costumes and had an affinity for Spanish Renaissance furniture. She heard a different drummer from the one who beat for most people before the First World War.

88, 89 The Frederic Douglass house in northeastern Washington was the suburban retreat – he owned a town house as well – of a former slave who became an important public official. The bedroom has a typical Victorian marble-topped dresser with kerosene lamp, flowered wash basin, and top hat.

90, 91, 92 An engraving of Abraham Lincoln (*left*) has a place of honor in the Frederick Douglass house; Douglass was a tireless crusader for the end of all traces of slavery. The dining room (*below*), with its cruet stand, colored ceiling lamp, bentwood armchair, is faithful to the late Victorian period, as is the room seen on the right.

93 The front porch of the Douglass house is bowered in old trees and faces an open lawn. Long preserved as a memorial by a group of black women's clubs and other admirers of Douglass' life, the house has more recently been restored by the Federal government and opened as a museum.

94, 95, 96 The Vice President's house (*right and below*) is a late Victorian mansion with curving verandahs, a pretty garden, informal furnishings and some young pine trees to screen it from the heavy traffic of Massachusetts Avenue. It shares an entrance drive, and a guard post, with the Naval Observatory.

97, 98, 99 The interior of the Victorian Toutorsky mansion (*left and below*) is one of the richest in Washington. The owner uses the house as a music academy as well as a dwelling; he and his wife acquired the house empty and have steadily added collections of a most catholic sort.

100, 101, 102, 103 The late Victorian drawing room of the Heurich Mansion (*above*) is virtually untouched since the 1890s. The ceiling cornice (*above right*), the minstrel gallery of the music room (*right*), the carving of the furniture are all superbly done in the opulent high style of the period.

104, 105 The Toutorsky house on Sixteenth Street was utterly bare when the family moved in 35 years ago. They were collecting things that delighted or amused them before that, and have continued to the present. Dr Toutorsky teaches a few students of the piano. His wife is especially fond of swans; there are about fifty of them here and there. The family are Russian, English and Spanish in origin, but they have drawn no hard lines in decor. Countless objects have comfortably moved in cheek by jowl in one of the capital's warmest and most astonishing houses.

106, 107, 108 Washington abounds in Victorian houses, like these three groups in different parts of the city. Even the row houses are marked by ingenuity of detail to avoid sterile sameness. The brickwork is always of high craftsmanship and frequently rewarding in the novelty of its design.

109 Two of the family's numerous swans remain adequately warm even in the quite cold Washington winters, doubtless encouraged by the Toutorsky house harp, the upright of which is just visible on the left.

110 The Heurich Mansion dining room is untouched since the end of the last century and is sometimes still used for quite grand luncheons given by the Columbia Historical Society, which uses the house for its headquarters. Apart from being a museum of late Victorian decor at its full-steam-ahead best, the building keeps archives of Washington history and occasionally displays such unexpected things as the small brandy glass used by Major Pierre L'Enfant (who laid out the capital) on his deathbed.

111 Many of the houses at Logan Circle (*above*) and in other temporarily unfashionable neighborhoods have been discovered as the treasures they are by space-hungry owners aghast at the cost of new housing.

112 Even smaller Victorian houses (*right*) are built with a solidity rarely thought of now. They have huge windows, high ceilings, big kitchens, pantries and other wonders. Increasing numbers of shops cater to the boom in the restoration business, providing contemporary hardware, woodwork, fireplace tiles, authentic paint colors and the like.

113, 114 Anderson House is a Massachusetts Avenue mansion built in 1905 for Larz Anderson, sometime minister to Belgium and ambassador to Japan. A marble hallway (*right*) parallels the parquet-floored ballroom through the arches, and a stair hall (*above*) suggests the general air of opulence, though not the effect, of the 30-foot-high ceilings of the main room. Now headquarters for a patriotic society the house displays historical porcelains, battle flags and important portraits of George Washington and Alexander Hamilton by Gilbert Stuart and Charles Willson Peale, respectively. Occasionally balls and dinners are given in this dazzling setting.

115, 116 A circular bay of stained glass in the Turkish Embassy (*above*) lights the splendid carpets and carved woodwork of this 1914 mansion. The stairway (*right*) is one of the richest in the city and the parquet floors are unusually fine. Off this large hall is a room with walls of embossed leather, which was popular in Washington at the time.

117 A handsome farmhouse was rebuilt into an approximation of Versailles for the Townsend family in 1899 (*left*). One of the most costly houses on Massachusetts Avenue, it was briefly occupied by President-elect Franklin Roosevelt and Mrs Roosevelt in 1933, and since 1950 has been home to the Cosmos Club, a town club for men chiefly in the learned professions.

118, 119 Meridian House (*right, above and below*) was built in 1922 for Irwin Laughlin, wealthy diplomat, by John Russell Pope, architect. Something of its general delicacy is seen in the railing and curvature of the stairs. It is now owned by Meridian House Foundation which has offices for various international service agencies concerned with foreign students, resident diplomatic families and the like. It is one of the last mansions built in the Sixteenth Street neighborhood.

The Turkish Embassy (*below and right*) is
one of several great mansions converted to
chanceries and residences of foreign ambassadors.
This splendid house at Sheridan Circle was among the
first to establish Massachusetts Avenue as the main
street for great embassies; earlier, Sixteenth Street
was the favored address.

122, 123, 124 The Miller mansion of 1901 was built for a Civil War naval officer and his wife, both of them with fortunes. The round towers and general fabric are brick, lavishly stone-trimmed, and it all looks as much like a small French château as anything else. The stone portico has an Italianate air and suggests the manner of Francis I, but the local architect, Paul Pelz, did not feel slavishly bound to any one system or style. The quite pleasant stone monster (*lower right*) serves as a gifted salamander, a modest dragon, or an adolescent sea monster and is merely one of many enchanting sculptural touches. The house is now the Argyle Guest House with rooms for rent. Motels in paradise are presumed to resemble it.

125 The Mexican Embassy is said to have been a wifely Christmas present to President Taft's treasury secretary in 1911. Secretary Franklin MacVeagh and his wife occupied it only until 1916 and it was then rented; the British prime minister and the Belgian king were guests then, and the Mexican government acquired it in 1921, but only occupied it in 1925.

126 An uncommonly large mural by Roberto Cueva del Rio lines the stair wall of the Mexican Embassy for three floors with dozens of figures illustrating both the history and society of the nation.

127 Often the pedestrian of the capital turns a corner to be dazzled by some house from another world, such as this Venetian fantasy escaped from the Grand Canal.

128, 129, 130 Anderson House, built in 1905 for a well-heeled American diplomat, is now a museum. The entrance portico is limestone (*above left*); the 30- by 80-foot ballroom (*below left*) is parquet, marble, wrought iron and crystal; the dining room (*right*) shares the general opulence.

131 The Cosmos Club's home on Massachusetts Avenue began as a Victorian farmhouse and was massively transformed into a town house with strong echoes of Versailles. Men notable in the learned professions eat, drink, entertain and get lectured to in its numerous stately rooms, and also read quietly in its library (*above*).

132 The Colombian Embassy is a wonderfully satisfying house of soft red brick and stone trim off Dupont Circle. Its iron porte cochère was once roofed with glass, scarcely needed, and not missed.

133, 134, 135 The Colombian Embassy's carved woodwork is notable even in a capital much given to whittling in the grand manner. However exuberant the details, the large expanses of paneled and plastered walls help to give a rather quiet and stately effect.

136 The ballroom (*above*) of the Colombian Embassy with its festive moulded and painted plaster lit by an airy dome contrasts strongly with the richly carved wood of the other public rooms.

137, 138 At Meridian House (*right and far right*) one of the grandest private dwellings of the town, now an international center at which families of resident foreign diplomats are made to feel at home, the Chinese influence in porcelain and chairs is combined with the mirrored walls and generally French decor. Outdoors, modern steel furniture looks attractive in the gravelled courtyard.

139, 140 A rightly uneasy ram peers from amid his carved stone grape vines at the rising tide of wisteria about to engulf him in the garden of Meridian House (*left*). Looking past the extremely busy cherubs (*below*) of Meridian House you can see the uncluttered sky and the stark fastigiate ginkgo.

141, 142 The Order of the Eastern Star, a fraternal organization, now owns the Perry Belmont mansion off Dupont Circle, but has left its 1909 decor virtually untouched. Marble halls (*left*) lead through columned openings into impressive suites. The Belmont staircase (*right*) promises that the top is worth getting to.

143, 144, 145, 146 The Belmont mansion was built by a Parisian architect, Sanson, and shows a fondness for eighteenth-century French style. An early twentieth-century telephone (*far right*) is discreetly housed in a globe. Sooner or later, when it starts jangling, you learn to pull South America away from Africa.

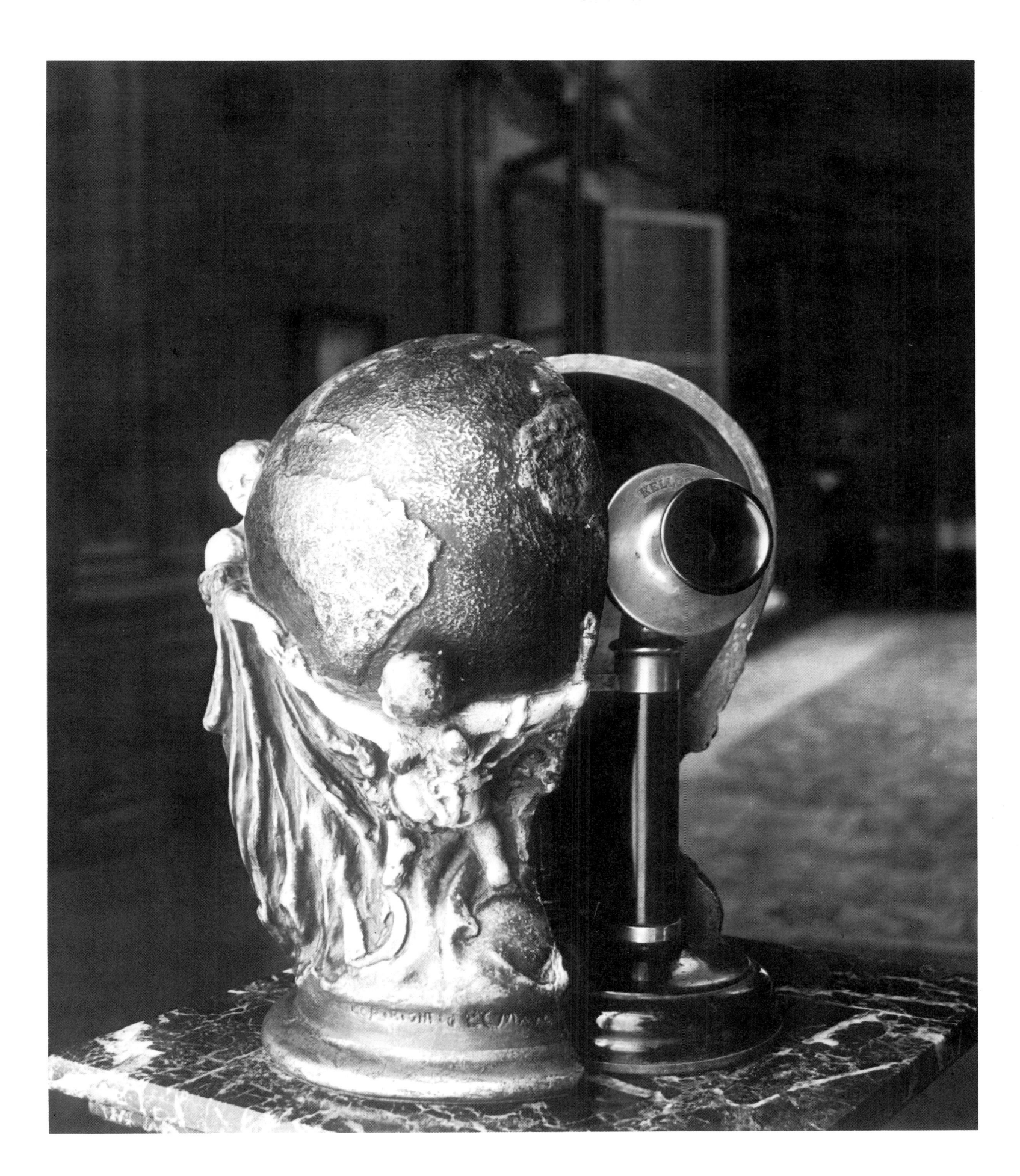

147, 148 The Washington Club (*left*) on Dupont Circle is a marble exercise in capital mansion-building. Originally occupied by the Patterson family, leaders in newspaper publishing, it is now a women's club in which members attend receptions, play bridge, hear lectures and flourish in general. A fireplace (*right*) keeps classical memories. President Coolidge entertained the aviator hero Charles Lindbergh in this house after the Paris flight.

149, 150, 151 The Brazilian Embassy (*left*) has the Neo-Classical repose associated with its architect, John Russell Pope, who built it in 1909 for Robert McCormick, diplomat, and his wife, a Medill of the Chicago publishing family. The Brazilian government bought the house in 1934. The façade suggests a Tuscan villa (*right*). Plants and flowers brighten the entrance hall (*below*) where the ceiling light is Brazilian silver; the iron stair railing is trimmed with rosewood.

153 The reception rooms of the Brazilian Embassy (*left*) are furnished with antiques and the walls are glorified with nineteenth-century romantic wallpaper showing the Brazilian countryside.

154 The red salon (*below*) of the Spanish Embassy is dominated by a Flemish tapestry of the seventeenth century and lights of Spanish crystal.

152 The marble stairs of the Brazilian Embassy (*left*) are railed in beautifully worked iron.

155 The Spanish Embassy was designed in 1923 by George Oakley Totten for Mary Henderson on Sixteenth Street, of which street Mrs Henderson was the greatest champion. It was offered to the American government as a house for the vice president, but was not accepted. The Spanish government bought it in 1926.

156 The Belgian Embassy was built in 1931 for an American millionaire family, the Bakers, and later occupied by the Palm Beach dowager, Mrs Edward T. Stotesbury, before the Belgians acquired it in 1945.

In the hall there are old porcelains, a Louis XV marble-topped table and a handsome railing of wrought and gilded iron.

157 The wrought-iron stairway in the ground-floor hall of the Russian Embassy on Sixteenth Street, built shortly before the Revolution, leads to a spacious suite upstairs, where large receptions are held.

158 The ballroom of the Russian Embassy has been the scene for such receptions as the one honoring both the Russian cosmonauts and the American astronauts.

149

159 Too often, when you see this house still standing, you greatly regret the one next to it that has been demolished.

160 The Sulgrave Club (*right*) was formerly a private dwelling with a huge entrance for carriages in the Massachusetts Avenue façade, now filled in. It is one of the city's most fashionable and elegant clubs for women. Quiet rooms like this one may be the scene for a reception honoring all living chiefs of protocol, at which unseemly noise is tolerated.

161 Dumbarton Oaks was built in 1801 and has been transformed both inside and out more than once, most recently by Robert Woods Bliss who in this century sheared off Victorian protuberances of singular ugliness. His wife collaborated from 1922 onwards for many years with the landscape gardener Beatrix Farrand.

162 The interior and exterior of the orangery at Dumbarton Oaks are equally inviting; the outside walls, built in 1801 or thereabouts, are hung with lavender wisteria. The interior posts seen through the open door are temporary supports for use while the roof is being prepared. (For the interior see Plate 169.)

163, 164 The Belmont house of 1909 (*opposite and top right*) retains its magnificent interior proportions and much of its original furnishing. The Parisian architect was let loose with Caen stone, mantels from various palaces, and a city block, and not surprisingly saw no reason to scrimp. The dining room was fitted with virtually everything but a Grand Canal, and the table seats 30 on Venetian velvet chairs.

165 The Belgian Embassy (*below*) was built in 1931 by a former American government official who clearly yearned for the seventeenth- and eighteenth-century hôtels of Paris. The Belgians bought the house in 1945 and serve strawberries at sun-struck spring luncheons.

166, 167 The gardens of Dumbarton Oaks (*below*) involve many changes of level, reached by admirably designed stairs, each of different character according to the formality or casualness of the immediate surroundings. The pebble garden is overlooked by iron-railed viewing spots. A cedar and weeping flowering cherry are planted back of the swimming pool garden. A carved stone vase (*right*) is typical of careful work in small details of the garden.

168 The pebble garden (*above*) is very lightly flooded to produce both a mirror and a colorful wet-seashell effect.

169 The interior of the orangery (*left*) is almost entirely taken over by a huge old creeping fig.

170 The music room (*right*) was added in 1929, and here in 1944 the Dumbarton Oaks Conference was held, presaging the United Nations Organization. The house and garden, set on extremely valuable Georgetown property, were given to Harvard University in 1940. Concerts are given here and garden symposia are held. The garden is possibly the most delightful of all those open to the public.

171, 172, 173 Staircases are a glory of many Washington mansions, though few are as astonishing as that of the Indonesian Embassy (*left and frontispiece*) which flaunts its Art Nouveau splendor in a three-storey glass-roofed entrance hall. It rises in one grand flight then divides into two ascending curves. The treads form a surreal pattern between the sweeping mahogany railings. The stairs of the Luxembourg Embassy (*above and right*) form beautiful if less complex patterns as they rise three floors.

174, 175 Among the pretentious houses of Sheridan Circle sits the modest (however costly) working studio of Alice Pike Barney who was born in the Mid-West in 1857. Mrs Barney studied painting abroad, with Whistler among others, and settled in Washington like a phoenix in a farm pasture, that is, she brought an exotic air with her. She had a great Washington mansion but this studio is more charming. It is now owned by the Smithsonian Institution.

176 Alice Pike Barney's studio (*left*) on Massachusetts Avenue is filled with Spanish furniture and paintings of her and by her. If there was to be furniture, Mrs Barney always felt there should be plenty of it. A liberated woman of the turn of the century, her five-storey studio was her serious toy. She also had a town mansion on another street.

177 The International Student House (*right*) off Dupont Circle was once a town mansion and now houses foreign students. The stairs lead from a great hall downstairs past this bay of leaded glass.

178, 179 The Italian Embassy staircase (*below right*) mounts with Jacobean solidity, but there is a sense of great space in the hall (*below*) with high beamed ceiling and gallery complete with pipe organ.

180 This rather exotic Victorian house exhibits some fine examples of Washington brickwork. It was recently threatened with demolition, but a public outcry saved it from the wreckers' ball.

181 Sixty foreign students now live in the International Student House at rates comparable to college dormitory housing. The hall with its beamed ceiling and stone fireplace is the main focal point. The mansion was given first to the American Friends Service Committee but now operates under its own board, whose members raise money each year to keep the house solvent.

The First World War and After

Whether the world went completely to pieces with the Great War of 1914–18 or whether that disaster ushered in a new order of the ages and a better one, this much is certain, a new pluralism, a new freedom, and some would say a new lack of discipline were almost instantly registered throughout the civilized world. Among Washington houses one has only to look at the Heurich Mansion of 1896 and the Woodrow Wilson House of 1915 to perceive what vast distances were traveled in so few years.

The Wilson House is a neo-Georgian three-storey town house occupied by the First World War president, Woodrow Wilson, and his second wife, Edith Bolling Galt, following his retirement in 1921. The president had been in poor health – his wife was severely criticized during his last term as president for possibly involving herself in decisions she had no authority to make – and Mrs Wilson found this dwelling and liked it. She considered it "an unpretentious, comfortable, dignified house suited to the needs of a gentleman," but she also thought it too costly, as houses of the sort usually are. The president bought it for her as a surprise, and she offered no further complaints about the cost. It was from this house, in 1924, that the president's body was taken on his death to Washington Cathedral, where his tomb may be seen off the nave.

The main rooms are on the second floor. The drawing room has an Empire sofa, a Georgian mantel, a handsome crystal chandelier, a lively carved mirror of partly Chippendale, partly Louis Philippe and partly Victorian persuasion, some fat Victorian sofas, a Federal mirror, and a reasonable assortment of bric-à-brac in the form of framed photographs (including one from King Edward VII and his Queen) and mementoes.

Mrs Wilson occupied the house until her death in 1961, and left it to the National Trust for Historic Preservation, which now maintains it as a museum. The president's bedroom is on the third floor, kept exactly as it was in 1924, with his pince-nez, his bathrobe and other personal belongings, and somewhat surprisingly the case of the first shell fired by American forces in the war. A copy of Thomas a Kempis' *Imitation of Christ* lies by the bedside.

182 In residential areas such as Cleveland Park a reasonably sober house may suddenly sprout a festive three-storey pagoda at its corner without batting an eye or making the least apology.

A floor clock on the stairs was acquired by Mrs Wilson when she learned the former president missed the chiming hours of the White House clock. The library (his personal library consisted of 8,000 books) is the site of his only radio broadcast (Armistice Day, 1923) and contains his ancient Victrola Talking Machine with its wooden needles.

Mrs Wilson was a descendant of Pocahontas – the seventeenth-century Indian "princess" who made rather a stir in London – and she therefore liked to surround herself with family pictures. She also enjoyed playing bridge in the sun room, and a bay window was added to catch the winter sun. The Wilsons also added a garage. The president's old car was a Pierce-Arrow; friends gave him a Rolls-Royce shortly before his death, but he rode in it only once. The old Otis elevator, installed for him, remains in the house as it was.

Until quite recently the American vice president had no official house; he laid his head where he could. From time to time fitful suggestions were made that this place or that would be nice for the vice president, but nothing came of them. Finally, when Rockefeller was vice president, the government acquired a white elephant of a house for the second-ranking official of the nation. Mr Rockefeller, while no doubt grateful, already had a much nicer house and his renovations of the new place (formerly the house of the chief of naval operations) were of such extent that he never got properly ensconced in it. The Rockefellers did acquire a brass bed costing $10,000, and for a time it was a talking point in the capital whether one had, or had not, dashed in to flop down on it for a second. Those who had, felt superior.

The official mansion now is done in a homey, semi-expensive style with slip covers and a general air that it is as comfortable as necessary. It is not, however, an inducement to run for high office, but then few Americans ever set out deliberately to become vice president. Indeed, the house serves admirably to remind any incumbent that he is of quite secondary importance and, moreover, usually the result of an uneasy compromise; with luck (if the president does not die in office) he will never be heard of again.

For all its high-tone Regency look, the Renchard house was built early in this century and improved substantially by the present owners. Once, when they were abroad, the house was rented by the American government as a guest house for visiting dignitaries while Blair House (which usually serves that purpose) was undergoing repairs and refurbishing.

The dining room is particularly satisfying – odd how often the dining room is the best room of a house – with full carved entablature and quite beautiful antique silver wall sconces from South America. The owner's bed, also an antique, is a magnificent South American masterpiece of great size. When the house was used by the visiting emperor of Ethiopia, he refused to sleep in it. He was of moderate stature and the bed would hold half his retinue. The chief of protocol had to arrange to have the bed

183 The birds of paradise above the mantel echo the informal elegance of the furnishings in Mrs Gordon Gray's handsome Washington home.

disassembled and removed while the emperor was dining with the president. Fortunately Mrs Renchard was out of the country at the time, otherwise she would have been greatly alarmed at the partial dismantling of her treasures. After the emperor left, the bed was safely returned, and put together again, much to the relief of the protocol officer no doubt.

While all houses are, of course, highly personal phenomena, one might hazard the hypothesis that before the First World War they were predictably in one style or another, even if it was only Victorian, while after that war houses came to display strongly personal aspects of the owner. Joseph Alsop's house in Georgetown, for example (which he rented when he sold his quite remarkable cinder-block dwelling stuffed with Chinese porcelains, Luristan bronzes, T'ang figurines and other pretty toys), was built in 1805 and was once owned by the Irish-born Thomas Corcoran, a rich leather merchant, mayor, and generally important citizen of the day, who came to America in 1783. The brickwork is especially neat, as the tight-jointed Flemish bond of Georgetown usually is, and the stone arch and keystone over the entrance doorway are fine examples of decoration carried just far enough and no farther. The fanlight is simple, sturdy, elegant, and nobody will ever feel the need to alter or improve it. The panels of the entrance door do not fully accord, some might say, with the perfect rightness of the rest of the façade. Why their designer could not leave plain rectangles alone cannot be ascertained; still, it is a trifling matter providing it does not make one too unhappy.

The 1805 date of Mr Alsop's house may seem suspiciously early for a post First World War dwelling. Inside, the house is so marked by the occupants' personal styles that – well, here it is, and may the wrath of Federal Georgetown not fall too heavily upon us.

Mr Alsop has been a political columnist for some decades. He is a cousin of President Franklin Roosevelt; he attended fashionable and good schools; and he must not be confused with those grubby newspaper folk who eat hamburgers and sport grimy nails. And yet the more a reporter differs from his fellows the more he illustrates the genre, since a tangential waywardness and a partial defiance of received wisdom have marked the American press since the eighteenth century, at least in its better moments. Mr Alsop has long fussed at the nation for not doing one thing or another, such as turning the Indian Ocean into an American lake or stopping the communists in Vietnam. Doom is regularly expected by his readers, and some day he will surely be proved correct; in the meantime, he is thought a major ornament of the town, where his fierce views on multicolored azaleas are as well known as his strictures on naval unpreparedness. He is rather a scholar, very much a connoisseur, and one of the few of his trade ever invited to deliver a series of prestigious lectures at the National Gallery on the collecting of art as a phenomenon of some

societies but not others.

His house is full of family pictures and others as well. He likes to be surrounded with familiar faces and on one wall has assembled so many that they serve as wallpaper. It is not thought feasible to have an important party in the town without Mr Alsop, and there he does not fuss, or fuss much, at other guests. His former wife, Susan Alsop, not merely knows everything going on in the capital, but is also a writer of ability and an extremely sharp observer of nuances and commonly overlooked details. She could be an American Pepys if she set her mind to it.

Hillwood is now a museum, but so it was when it was occupied by Mrs Merriweather Post, heiress to a great cereal fortune, whose very cemetery for family dogs (with its weeping dogwoods, dog-tooth violets, etc.) is handsomer than most gardens. The house is a treasury of magnificent French, Russian and English objects of great luxury. The entrance hall has a marble Louis XVI table on which stands a marble bust of one of Louis XV's mistresses, affording a nice sense of continuity. The stair wall is lined with portraits of czars, czarinas and other members of the imperial family. Few things illustrate better than this magnificent entrance hall the royal place of cornflakes in the American diet.

The rooms are a succession of precious porcelains (four services made for Catherine the Great, some Sèvres made for Mme de Pompadour), furniture given to a prince by Louis XVI, jeweled Fabergé trinkets, Beauvais tapestries from Boucher designs, chairs by Georges Jacob, an Aubusson rug intended for Maximilian and Carlotta (and in storage for seventy-five years), and vastly rich chalices and icons. By the time one gets to mere Sheraton and Queen Anne and Georgian treasures, even the Grinling Gibbons carving seems routine enough.

Descending from imperial heights to earth again, the house of former Mayor and Mrs Walter Washington is a study in solid unpretentious American house-building.

Mrs Dean Acheson's Georgetown house has such touches as curtains on the wooden window louvers and, although the house is old, a polished tile floor with lots of sun and plenty of plants. Her late husband, the Secretary of State, shared her love of gardening and himself rooted the box bushes (now large) of their country place. Mrs Acheson is one of the town's best conversationalists, provided she is not expected to deal in small talk and social chatter, which have no appeal for her.

Mrs Duncan Phillips possesses in her dining room one of the few Picasso paintings ever mistaken for a Corot, and in the drawing room a Bonnard that may stand for the ultimate Bonnard. A hallway is shielded by a beautiful Prendergast screen. Everything in the house is serene, uncrowded, unemphasized and satisfying. Nothing is loud or jarring except the exuberant schnauzer who sits semi-obediently at his mistress's chair and eats unauthorized shrimps.

When she was a bride in her twenties, Mrs Phillips dined with her

184 Mirrors are an important feature in this 1940s house.

173

husband at the apartment of the dealer Durand-Ruel in Paris, and the huge and marvelous Renoir *Luncheon of the Boating Party* was hung especially to tempt her. She and her husband bought it virtually on sight, a rare instance of a young woman discovering and walking off with a master-piece, which is now a major treasure of the Phillips Collection.

In the 1920s the Phillipses turned their old Dupont Circle mansion into an art gallery, perhaps the world's first such gallery for "modern" art. In no time at all, of course, the paintings (they are not all modern: there are superb Grecos, a great Daumier, a surprisingly tender Delacroix, and so on) and the visitors drove the Phillipses out, to the present mansion twenty minutes from downtown.

185 A handsome chair sets off a corner of a room with a 1930s flavor in Mrs Phillips' house.

Mrs Phillips is now well past eighty, but continues to entertain. Invitations to her small, low-keyed parties are eagerly accepted by the lucky. Since she suffers from cold feet she has turned her back on the follies of fashionable shoes and invested in some good warm galoshes; she wears one or another pair of them with all her costumes and has been relatively comfortable, thank you, ever since.

Senator and Mrs Pell's house is a notable mansion of 1798 which long stood empty but is now handsomely restored with a strong individual taste. There are a number of twentieth-century portraits and many mementoes of earlier centuries. One of the senator's forbears, Sir John Pell (of Pelham Manor, New York, in 1687), is represented in a handsome portrait, as indeed is the first American-bred horse to win the English Derby, a splendid beast called Iroquois owned by the senator's collateral relative, Pierre Lorillard, of Tuxedo Park and tobacco. Senator Pell is one of the most visible legislators of the capital, and few live in a house so picturesquely identified with the town's past.

The house was pretty much in ruins until taken in hand by Lady Lewis during the Second World War (her husband was Sir Wilmott Lewis of *The Times* of London). Some of the floor planks, which are forty feet long, required bracing, and the roof was a ruin, as were the watered interior walls. One way and another Mrs Lewis succeeded in putting the old house together again. It is still known locally as the Worthington House after that doughty physician who was given a gold snuff box by some wounded British soldiers in 1812. An appropriate gift since he was rather a dandy in his personal garb. Another owner of the house moved in from the remote countryside long enough to marry off his daughter, ruinously described as "sensible," then retired to his farm again. Yet another owner, possibly a trifle eccentric, acquired a great many seats from Ford's Theater and stored them up on the third floor of the house. The daughter of one family in this house married a young man who had been designated successor to Maximilian, the Emperor of Mexico, but who sensibly stayed put in Washington.

As a foil to too many notable houses of too many notable people, one may mention the Mitchell Mansion (as it is called), which measures twenty by thirty feet over-all and is occupied by a hard-working newspaper fellow of low rank in town. The house illustrates two relevant points: it was built in 1931 and the porch could easily have come from a seventeenth-century Virginia farmhouse, the stairway from a Georgetown house of 1810 – as late as the Great Depression it did not occur to the local builder that there was anything odd or anachronistic in this; secondly, the house is largely furnished with stuff from family attics and houses of larger scale. The houses of Washington tend to blossom with dining tables, mirrors, pictures, chandeliers, and no telling what else, all dutifully retrieved from some place or other, the armchairs often bearing the teeth marks of hounds long dead

175

(in dark Southern houses a good bit of chewing can be accomplished before anybody notices it). The coarse wooden food safe, which always sat in a Tennessee barn, does not go well with a portable Renaissance chest inlaid with ivory, which looks odd beneath the framed pages of the Nuremberg Chronicle, and none of them looks right with the big Havell aquatint of marsh birds. Still, there it is, all mixed up sufficiently to give a decorator nightmares, but such is life, and such are many Washington houses.

The Claytor House, a typical Federal house on the outside, with a quite pretty fanlight, possesses a fine collection of model trains as well as Mrs Claytor's extensive collection of dolls. Personal enthusiasms have to go somewhere, after all, and the householders of Washington, like others elsewhere, commonly trail their past lives with them when they move. (Mr Claytor was a railroad president before he was Secretary of the Navy.)

One of the most conspicuous women of the town is Kay Graham, chairman of The Washington Post Company. Her parents and her late husband began the nerve-racking task of converting a lesser newspaper into one that, at least in the view of liberals, may be called a good one. To the surprise of a great many people, it was only when the total responsibility for the newspaper fell into the hands of an inexperienced woman that the paper entered its period of greatest prosperity and, not to split hairs, importance.

Mrs Graham is one of the city's high-voltage hostesses. Conversation at her house is said to be brilliant or awesome or both, and people commonly report they have met Saint Luke and the Devil himself at her suppers, along with less resplendent mortals. Her house is a Victorian mansion in Georgetown, sufficiently large for some people to mope at not being invited there. It's not as if it held only four couples.

Washington does seem, sometimes, to be populated by important hostesses and grandes dames, who maintain they are just having a few friends in, and who, moreover, are far too young to be insulted by being called grandes anything. But there they are, all the same, Mesdames Burling, Cooper, Fritchie and Charles among them. Their houses are notable chiefly because they inhabit them.

Mr Quirk's residence is somewhat smaller than most Washington town houses. It is eleven feet two inches wide. He himself, needless to say, is uncommonly tall and athletic. He is a young lawyer, formerly a member of the honor guard at Arlington, the national cemetery; he is among the few ever accidentally to fall backwards into an open grave as mourners assembled beneath the tent. One may have awkward days in the capital, but resilience is the keyword here. Those who recover may expect to survive; a thought that occurs to one, observing Mr Quirk at his ease in his compact Georgetown castle, or admiring the blue water lilies in the Long Water – a watering trough for horses, elevated to this beautiful use – in his garden at the back.

186 Mrs Charles' house is the scene of many delightful Washington gatherings, and in this corner one could converse very comfortably.

187, 188, 189 When President Woodrow Wilson retired from office, his wife (in portrait at left) thought this house would be suitable for a gentleman and so it proved, once the sunny bay (*right*) was added; it was a setting for many bridge games. The stair landing (*below*) holds a floor clock acquired by the Wilsons because the president missed the chiming clocks of the White House.

190, 191, 192 The Woodrow Wilson house, now a museum, is filled with mementoes. Edith Bolling Galt Wilson was as feminine as she was forceful; her taste for luxurious fabrics is seen here and there (*left*) and she saw no reason to repose on hard benches. A reasonable assortment of hatpins is ready for action on a dressing table (*above*). One of the touching reminders of the difficult First World War days is a figure representing the Red Cross (*right*), displaying what now seems a quite advanced and offensive bathos, but widely admired in its time as art, and now as a memorial of suffering.

193, 194, 195 Until Miss Grace Fox (*above*) sold her house in 1981, she had lived in it for almost seventy years. The entrance hall (*left*) retains its inlaid floor, its sturdy stairway and its homey old radiator. Most of the furniture was installed in 1913 and not much changed since.

196, 197 The Renchard house was built in 1905 and substantially remodeled later. A restraint suggestive of early Regency houses is clear in its façade (*above*). Its furnishings (*left*) are chiefly antique, collected over many years and catholic in origin. The house was used by visiting foreign guests of the president while Blair House was repaired during the Kennedy administration.

198, 199, 200 At the British Embassy, designed by Lutyens for that use, the garden portico pavement uses thin gray slates set on edge (*right*), a seemingly fragile device that has nevertheless proved quite practical over the decades. Guests arriving for the numerous social events held at the embassy – many of them to benefit charities – use these steps (*below*) to reach the reception rooms upstairs. Beyond the flying bridge a large portrait of King George III is just visible on the landing. A hall of polished stone (*below right*) leads through the main rooms. The magnificent Chinese lidded vases are on occasion replaced with great masses of flowers.

201, 202, 203 President Woodrow Wilson and his second wife, Edith Bolling Galt, moved into this town house in 1921. Edith Wilson chose the house, not wanting something too grand, but something suitable for a gentleman, and the president bought it for her. It was built in 1915, a red-brick, neo-Georgian affair to which the Wilsons added iron gates and a garage and installed an elevator. The house is furnished with objects of sentimental value to the Wilsons. After Mrs Wilson's death in 1961 the house passed to the National Trust for Historic Preservation as a museum. President Wilson died in the bedroom (*right*) which is kept as he left it.

188

204, 205, 206 A quiet house in Georgetown (*below*) is occupied by Alice Acheson, widow of Secretary of State Dean Acheson. A sunny fresh country look pervades a hall and is enhanced by the use of polished rough floors, fluffy curtains, large windows and many plants (*right*). Mrs Acheson long enjoyed an old country farmhouse near Washington with her husband, who rooted much of the extensive boxwood there from cuttings. In the city she remains a fond gardener, giving a hybrid hippeastrum (*left*) a spot in bright sun to ripen its foliage.

207, 208 The house of Miss Grace Fox, in which she lived 67 years, was sold recently. The warm wood trim of the living room (*right*), its beamed ceiling and its Jacobean furniture have never been changed, though some new furniture was acquired for the dining room before 1920. The entrance hall and a reception room (*left*) show the white paint and natural wood of the period. The inlaid border of the floors, which looks like mosaic tile, is in fact mahogany and other woods in a Greek key fret. Apart from a new furnace and some non-antique light bulbs in the lamps, the house is just as it always was.

209, 210, 211 Former Mayor Walter Washington (*left*) was the first mayor of the capital in modern times. Formerly the city was governed by commissioners chosen by Congress. He and Mrs Washington live in an old-fashioned house with polished wood floors and plain, quiet walls for restful background (*below*). A modern pedestal table (*right*) contrasts handsomely with the old gleaming wood of the stairway.

212 The great estate of Hillwood (*above*), home of Mrs Merriweather Post, is now a museum filled with French eighteenth-century furniture and other treasures, including many from Czarist Russia, as well as important collections of porcelain.

213 A charming aspect of many Washington houses is the small town garden, like this one of Mrs Poe Burling in Georgetown (*left*).

214 The British Embassy is the only house in the capital designed by Sir Edwin Lutyens, a very British architect. It was designed to look like an English country house. The grand porch, where guests sit, is not actually the entrance.

215 The Renchard town house has many splendid antiques, including this great bed from Ecuador (*right*). Haile Selassie, the Ethiopian emperor, refused to sleep in it when he stayed here as guest of the American government, complaining that it was too big.

216 A great spreading porch roof tends to the summer sun in a Cleveland Park house (*left*).

217, 218 Senator and Mrs Claiborne Pell live in a historic house in Georgetown (*above and above right*), very Southern in style, filled with family possessions from the seventeenth century on.

219 A rather fabulous Victorian porch leads into the Charles house (*below right*), presided over by one of the city's fashionable and witty hostesses.

220 Senator and Mrs Claiborne Pell have turned a locally celebrated house of the Federal period into a warm and personal place full of family mementoes of several centuries (*below*). In this house an early owner treated British wounded at the Battle of Bladensburg in the War of 1812.

221 The Claytor house stair railings (*right*) are Chinese fretwork of a sort greatly admired in eighteenth-century America.

222, 223, 224 A reeded mantelpiece (*left*) in the Claytor house in Georgetown holds a collection of shells among the more usual ornaments beneath the ubiquitous picture of George Washington. Former Secretary of the Navy William Claytor was president of a major railroad and the house is full of toy trains (*below left*), some of them about to run off the mantel. A Victorian doll-house (*right*) brings a dollop of giddiness to a room of eighteenth-century furniture.

225 The galleries of the Cooper house in Georgetown command an unusually large town garden and collect whatever summer breeze is stirring.

226, 227 The Burling house (*right and far right*), also in Georgetown, is beautifully filled with old furniture. Through an unusual and handsome door frame a post-Federal elevator forms an engaging pattern with the staircase.

228 The library of Mrs John Sherman Cooper's house.

229 Mrs Duncan Phillips (*right*) keeps her Foxhall Road house full of flowers. A drawing-room door opens into the library, where Marjorie Phillips is standing, with the dining room behind that. When the door is closed, the magnificent Prendergast screen is drawn across it on the drawing-room side.

230, 231 A bedroom fireplace wall (*left*) in the Georgetown house of columnist Joseph Alsop blooms forth with family photographs and other personal relics. The columnist's dining room (*below left*) is warmed by an old fireplace. The old paneling sets off the large portraits, and the elegant Empire lines of the furniture provide a lighter touch.

232 The large Victorian Georgetown house of
Katharine Graham, chairman of The Washington
Post Company, includes an unusually beautiful
fireplace and furniture arranged for small
conversational groups.

233 Susan Mary Alsop's handsome old French
furniture in her Georgetown house (*below*) is
enhanced by flowers everywhere and a chaste
mantelpiece flanked by old Chinese porcelain vases.

234, 235 Columnist and connoisseur Joseph Alsop (*far left*) once lived in a remarkable small house filled with Chinese treasures, but now resides in a Federal house in Georgetown filled with mementoes of a long career. He still writes, lectures occasionally, and maintains a wide circle of important friends. Susan Mary Alsop, formerly his wife, lives in another Georgetown house remarkable for style and polish (*left*).

236 Katharine Graham (*above*), chairman of The Washington Post Company, lives in a Victorian mansion in Georgetown, and is often hostess at small sparkling parties.

237 The Mitchell house (*left*) in American University Park is a cottage-sized house of 1930, interesting for the obsolete construction scheme of plaster applied directly to solid brick walls. The house is furnished from family attics and an earlier house in Tennessee.

238 Occasionally one sees a quite plain house with some stunning detail like the refined little Doric portico (*below*) of this clapboard dwelling.

239 The Quirk house in Georgetown is only 11 feet wide (*right*), yet the owner has managed not only a paved sitting place in the garden but an arbor of grapes and clematis, and a small pool for fish and water lilies as well.

240, 241 The Gordon Gray living room is typical of informal elegant Washington rooms in which comfortable stuffed furniture mixes with Chippendale mahogany beneath eighteenth-century entablatures to produce a confident, cheerful, unpretentious setting (*above and left*).

242 Columnist Clayton Fritchey and his wife live in a splendid Georgetown mansion with a particularly lovely garden overflowing with greenery (*right*) where they enertain during the long season of fine warm weather.

Acknowledgements

Henry Mitchell, Derry Moore, and John Calmann and Cooper Ltd wish to express their thanks to those listed below who so gladly cooperated in the preparation of this book for publication. A special debt of gratitude is owed to Mary Henderson, whose idea the book was in the first place, and a particular word of appreciation to Mrs Nancy Reagan for allowing us to photograph the White House.

Mrs Dean Acheson
Mr Joe Alsop
Mrs Susan Mary Alsop
Mr Charles Atherton
Ms Teresa Brown
Mrs Ella Poe Burling
Mrs Robert Charles
Mrs William Claytor Jr.
Mr Clement Conger
Mrs John Sherman Cooper
Mr Perry Fisher
Miss Grace Fox
Mr James M. Goode
Mrs Katharine Graham
Mrs Gordon Gray
Mr Ed Jones
Mr Bob Kaiser
Mr Lawrence Kolp
Mrs David Morse
Mrs Claiborne Pell
Mr & Mrs Armistead Peter 3rd
Mrs Duncan Phillips

Ms Judy Sobel
Dr & Mrs Basil Toutorsky
Mayor & Mrs Walter Washington

The staff of:
Bacon House
Barney House
Belgian Embassy
Belmont House
Blair House
Brazilian Embassy
Colombian Embassy
Columbia Historical Society
Cosmos Club
Decatur House
Dumbarton Oaks
Frederick Douglass House
Indonesian Embassy
International Student House
Luxembourg Embassy
Meridian House
Mexican Embassy
National Society of Colonial Dames
Octagon House
Russian Embassy
Spanish Embassy
Sulgrave Club
Turkish Embassy
Vice President's House
Washington Club
Woodrow Wilson House

Index